HUMAN RELATIONS:
THE BASIS FOR SUCCESS
IN THE WORKPLACE

CLAUDE P. MAJOR, Ph.D.

DARNLEY PUBLISHING GROUP

Legal deposit – Bibliothèque et Archives nationales du Québec, 2009
Legal deposit – Library and Archives Canada, 2009

ISBN 978-2-923623-39-9

Printed in Canada

TBCA1-5

Author: Claude P. Major, Ph.D.

Editor-in-chief: Alison Piper, M.A. (Ed. Tech.)

Copy Editor: Matthew Testa, M.A.

Project Manager: Francine Hébert, M. Ed.

Design and Layout: Rasha Razzak

Table of Contents

SECTION I: SOCIAL BEHAVIOR

Chapter 1   What Is Social Studies?   5

Chapter 2   The Foundations of Human Behavior   15

Table of Contents

| **Chapter 3** | **The Process of Socialization** | **33** |

Table of Contents

Table of Contents

Table of Contents

Table of Contents

Introduction

The human relations field examines how people relate to each other in group situations, especially at work, and how communication skills and sensitivity to other people's feelings can be improved. You could say that human relations is the study of how to relate successfully to other people, because the field is concerned with improving relationships between people and within groups. Why is learning about human relations essential to achieving success in the workplace?

Companies need employees who are able to:

- communicate and convey information effectively,

- interpret others' emotions,

- be open to others' feelings, and

- resolve conflicts and arrive at resolutions.

By acquiring these skills, you as an employee will be able to maintain more compatible relationships with colleagues, customers, your supervisor, and others whom you deal with at work.

This book will help you understand how to build successful relationships with others and to improve your human relations skills. The topics selected for study here are designed to help you achieve success in your working life. However, the human relations skills described here can be applied to all aspects of life, not just to the workplace. We can also benefit greatly from successful relationships with family members, friends, and others who are important to us in our personal lives.

Organization of the Text

This book is divided into two sections. Section I, "Social Behavior," will provide you with the background necessary to understand the behavior, feelings, and motivations of others. It covers such topics as human behavior, psychology, and social development. Section II, "Achieving Human Relations Success," discusses the attitudes and behaviors that lead to successful relationships in the workplace and success in general. It covers how to build and maintain relationships with coworkers and deal with problems you can expect to encounter at work.

Section I: Social Behavior

In chapter 1, "What Is Social Studies?" you will be introduced to some of the social science disciplines human relations draws from, including psychology, sociology, and business management.

In chapter 2, "The Foundations of Human Behavior," you will find out about the factors that shape and influence how people behave.

Chapter 3, "The Process of Socialization," describes the socialization process we go through to learn how to participate with others in our society.

Chapter 4, "Social Issues in General," covers the social issues that shape the world around us, including poverty, alcoholism and drug abuse, domestic violence, and racism.

Chapter 5, "Social Issues in the Workplace," will help you understand the subtleties of the work environment and the social issues that concern the workplace directly. These include discrimination, absenteeism, and sexual harassment.

Section II: Achieving Human Relations Success

In chapter 6, "Attitudes That Promote Human Relations Success," you will learn about the attitudes and strategies that lead to successful interpersonal relationships with employers, colleagues, and clients.

Chapter 7, "Stress and Frustration," discusses how to cope with stress in the workplace effectively and how to maintain a healthy, balanced lifestyle.

Chapter 8, "Common Errors in the Workplace," describes common errors people make when interacting with others at work, and how to avoid these problems.

Chapter 9, "Mistakes and Adversity," discusses the importance of admitting to mistakes in the workplace and how to do so in a professional manner that preserves your integrity. It also covers how to handle adversity in the workplace effectively and professionally. Workplace adversity may include conflicts and confrontations with angry coworkers and disagreements with a supervisor.

Because we can't do our jobs alone, chapter 10, "Getting Help," discusses the importance of accepting help from others when you need it and building alliances with the coworkers with whom you work regularly. It also covers self-motivation—how you can give back to a workplace team by taking initiative and making your own important contributions.

Features

This book contains the following features to facilitate the acquisition and review of key information:

Highlights of the Chapter. Each chapter begins with a list of the topics to be covered in the chapter.

Key Terms. Each chapter includes short definitions of the key terms used in the text, for ready reference.

Chapter Summaries. Chapters end with a brief summary, which will help you tie together the content of each chapter.

SECTION I: SOCIAL BEHAVIOR

CHAPTER 1

What Is Social Studies?

Highlights of the Chapter

This Chapter Covers:

- An introduction to a few of the subjects covered in social studies: psychology, sociology, and business management

- General qualities of a socially well-adjusted person

Social studies is the examination of how people interact in our society. It covers many subject areas, one of the most important of which is human relations. Human relations is a study of what our society expects of us, and how we can become successful and satisfied members of it.

Human relations involves a lot more than what to say or not to say, how to follow instructions or be accountable to a supervisor, or guidelines for courtesy or tactfulness. It addresses the fundamental issues of who we are, how we interact with other human beings around us, and the root causes of both successes and failures in our interactions.

It also helps us:

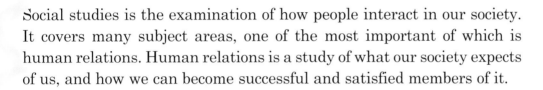

- Understand how viewpoints, beliefs, fears, insecurities, and hostile feelings take shape in us and in others.

- Understand our own motivations and those of others around us.

- Be sensitive to other people's points of view.

The field of human relations is vast and complex. There are many different viewpoints from which to study it. The topics selected for study here are designed to help you achieve success in your working life. However, the human relations skills described here can be applied to all aspects of life, not just to the workplace.

Human relations as a subject area draws from several different social studies disciplines, including psychology, sociology, and business management. This chapter explains what each of these fields covers, and who the professionals are who practice in these areas. This will help make it clear to you where to turn for additional information or assistance in any area that may be of particular significance to you.

This chapter also describes the general qualities of a socially well-adjusted person, to give you an understanding of what makes people succeed or fail in work, social situations, and life in general.

Subjects Covered in Social Studies

Psychology

Psychology is the study of the mind and its effects on human behavior. It is classified as a social science. There is a scientific component involving testing and field studies, but also a theoretical element that interprets the science and is open to debate and discussion. Psychology looks at human development from infancy through all phases of life. It examines fears, feelings, behaviors, and motivations. It describes what is needed for normal and successful human development, and what elements can interfere in this process and create problems.

A person with a graduate degree in psychology is called a psychologist. Some psychologists teach or do clinical research on the scientific aspects of behavior. Other psychologists act as counselors and work with clients who are experiencing developmental problems or behavior-related difficulties.

Psychologists versus Psychiatrists

Many people have trouble understanding the distinction between psychologists and psychiatrists. Psychiatry is the medical study of abnormal mental or emotional conditions and disorders. Unlike a psychologist, a psychiatrist is a medical doctor. This means that he or she has gone through medical school before obtaining specialized training in psychiatry. Because a psychiatrist is a medical doctor, he or she can prescribe drugs and medical treatments for which a psychologist has no license or training.

Since many psychiatrists provide therapy and counseling to patients, some aspects of their work overlap with the work of psychologists. A person with no specific disorder that requires medical treatment might receive help from either a psychologist or a psychiatrist. However, patients with serious or complex mental or emotional problems, such as schizophrenia, are usually treated by a psychiatrist.

The distinction is important because many mental disorders or problems can be triggered or aggravated by chemical or hormonal imbalances in the brain. It has recently been learned that some forms of depression, as well as attention deficit problems in children, fall into this category. A person suffering from such a condition may need medical treatment with drugs or special therapies in order to have the best chance of recovery. Counseling alone may not be sufficient.

Sociology

Sociology is the study of the structure and functioning of human society. It focuses more on trends in group behavior than on individual development. Because it is also a social science, it has developed objective research methods. Sociologists examine issues such as urbanization, changes to population groups, causes and patterns of poverty or crime, and government responses to social problems.

A social worker is a person employed by a government department, or occasionally by a charity or private corporation, whose job is to assist individuals who are experiencing social problems. Social workers intervene in cases where people are suffering from social injustice or abuse. They arrange for needy persons to receive social assistance and to participate in government-sponsored programs. Social workers often have a background in sociology. Many of them also have a postgraduate degree from a school of social work.

Business Management

Business management is an applied social science that focuses specifically on human relations in the workplace. Schools of business management train people who are destined to fulfill management roles within corporations and government departments. They also conduct research and experiments that are concerned with leadership, guidance, discipline, security, creativity, safety, and personal satisfaction within the workplace.

The General Qualities of a Socially Well-Adjusted Person

In this text we draw together ideas, information, and examples from all of these various fields. Human behavior has been closely and systematically studied by the social sciences for over 100 years. We have gained a good understanding of what makes most people succeed or fail in social situations generally, and the workplace in particular. Psychologists can explain behavior and its outcomes in a wide range of situations.

There are always exceptions to every rule. As human beings, we are not stamped out of a mold, identical and totally predictable. Free will and individual choice are important parts of our human constitution. However, we are all influenced by predisposing factors far more than most of us realize. Without an understanding of these factors, we may not be as free and as self-directed as we think we are.

When we use the term "success" in this text, we are referring to more than just money. In a broader sense, a successful person is someone whose life is "working well" from their point of view and that of most of the people around them. A person's life can be going well even if he or she does not have a great deal of money. Conversely, a person may have a high income but may in other important areas be facing serious difficulties.

In general it can be said that a person's life is going well if they possess most or all of the following qualities:

- Economically they have basic comforts and feel reasonably secure, whatever their standard of living.

- They are employed in some line of work that makes them feel productive and competent, even if that work is not high-paying, technically complex, or wildly exciting.

- They have at least a few stable and satisfying personal relations with parents, siblings, spouses, lovers, or close friends.

- They participate in society in a way that is acceptable to society itself; in other words they are not in conflict with the world around them and do not face arrests, evictions, or dismissals, and they are also neither the victims nor perpetrators of violent acts or serious antisocial behaviors.

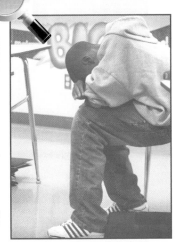

■ Their health is generally good, or at least they do not display health problems that are caused or aggravated by stress, conflict, depression, anxiety, or confusion.

They are not happy all of the time—no one is—but when they are not experiencing a moment of specific illness or crisis, they are fundamentally content with who they are and with life itself. They have a strong will to live and hopes for the future.

It is more difficult to make progress when one has been the victim of domestic instability, abuse, economic disadvantage, illness, accidents, or serious mistakes during one's upbringing or recent past. This is why people with specific or urgent social problems should always seek professional assistance.

Fulfilling everything on the above list is a tall order. No book could ever hope to hold the answers to all of life's problems and challenges. There is no adequate substitute for learning from real-life experiences.

Learning how to become a successful and contented human being is a lifelong process. Nevertheless, there are several fundamental attitudes and skills that help most people to get started in the right direction and make sure and steady progress.

Summary

The human relations field studies how people relate to each other in group situations, especially at work, and how communication skills and sensitivity to other people's feelings can be improved. It draws from several different social studies disciplines, including psychology, sociology, and business management.

Psychology is the study of human development and behavior. Psychiatry is the study of abnormal mental or emotional conditions and disorders. Psychiatrists and psychologists may both provide therapy; however, unlike a psychologist, a psychiatrist is a medical doctor who can prescribe drugs and medical treatments. Patients with serious or complex mental or emotional problems are usually treated by a psychiatrist.

Sociology is the study of the structure and functioning of human society. It focuses more on trends in group behavior than on individual development.

Business management is an applied social science that focuses specifically on human relations in the workplace. Schools of business management train people to fill management roles within corporations and government departments.

Key Terms

Term	Definition
Business management	Business management is an applied social science that focuses specifically on human relations in the workplace. Schools of business management train people to fulfill management roles within corporations and government departments.
Business manager	Business managers hold management positions in corporations and government departments. They may be hired to manage a company's business functions and help ensure its profitability.
Human relations	The human relations field studies how people relate to each other in group situations, especially at work, and how communication skills and sensitivity to other people's feelings can be improved.
Psychiatrist	Psychiatrists are medical doctors with specialized training in the treatment of mental disorders, including mental illnesses, severe learning disabilities, and personality disorders.
Psychiatry	Psychiatry is a branch of medicine that exists to study, prevent, and treat mental disorders in humans.
Psychologist	Psychologists are experts in psychology who provide mental health care and conduct research.
Psychology	Psychology is the study of the human mind and its effects on behavior.
Social studies	Social studies is the examination of how people interact in our society. It covers many subject areas, one of the most important of which is human relations.

Term	Definition
Social worker	Social work is the profession committed to the pursuit of social justice, to the enhancement of the quality of life, and to the development of the full potential of each individual, group, and community in society.
Social work	A social worker is a person employed by a government department, a charity, or a private corporation to assist those who are experiencing social problems, social injustice, or abuse. They may work with individuals, families, groups, organizations, and communities.
Sociologist	A sociologist is a social scientist who specializes in sociology. Sociologists study the institutions and structure of human society.
Sociology	Sociology is the study of the structure and functioning of human society.

CHAPTER 2

The Foundations of Human Behavior

Highlights of the Chapter

This Chapter Covers:

- How our genes and our social upbringing shape who we are
- The nature of human emotions
- The motives that influence our behavior
- Freud's theories of the human mind
- The defense mechanisms we commonly use to avoid difficult and stressful situations

Introduction

Many of us have wondered about our unique lives and identities: Who are we? What are we like? How did we get to be this way? Is there anything we can do to improve the situation?

These questions cannot be answered by intuition and opinion alone. Just as there is a scientific element to biological man, there is also a scientific element to the social process that has produced us and brought us to the present point in our lives. In order to understand ourselves, we must begin by looking at the science of our lives.

We now know a great deal about human development and how the human mind works. By studying other people and society as a whole, we can discover what works and what doesn't work for others, and why. There is a good chance that much of what applies to others will also apply to ourselves.

This chapter covers the foundations of human behavior, including the extent to which genetics and our upbringing and environment shape

our personality, social skills, and the social problems that we will experience during our lives. This chapter also examines the nature of human emotions, what motivates us to behave the way we do, and the defense mechanisms we commonly use to avoid difficult situations that cause stress and anxiety. Freud's theories of the human mind are included to provide a model of how the mind might work and help explain why we find it so difficult to understand our own thought processes.

Nature versus Nurture

Psychologists and other social scientists who study human behavior attempt to understand just what kind of factors affect who a person turns out to be. They want to determine how much of personality and behavior can be explained by biological causes, and how much can be attributed to social upbringing. In the field of psychology, there has been a long-standing debate between those who believe that nature determines who we are and those who believe that what we experience and learn as children is all that matters. We call this the nature-versus-nurture debate.

Today, few social scientists believe that only nature or only nurture determines who we are. It is generally accepted that both the internal biology we inherit and the social environment we grow up in shape who we become. In other words, the nature we are born with and the nurture we experience are both responsible for why we are the way we are.

Nature: Our Genetics

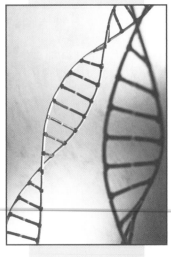

When we talk about an individual's "nature," we refer mainly to genetics. Humans, like all living things, contain a set of genes inside every one of their living cells. These genes contain a long and complex set of instructions for how cells and parts of the body are to grow and develop. They directly determine physiological features, such as our overall size, our sex, our hair and eye color, and our skin color. They also play an important role in determining some of the brain's many capabilities.

Because half of our genetic material comes from each parent, we inherit many of our parents' traits. Thus we bear some resemblance to our biological parents, even if they are not the ones who raise us through childhood. We also share many genes with our brothers and

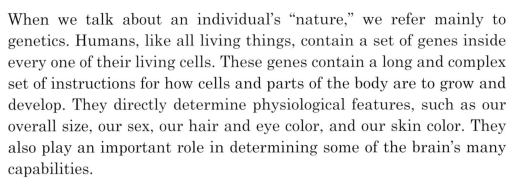

sisters. However, only identical twins have exactly the same genetic material as each other.

Genes also contribute to our behavior in many ways, one of which is through instinct. An instinct is an innate tendency to behave in a certain way, usually one that is essential to survival. Instincts are especially important in animal behavior, but they also help humans survive. For example, a baby does not need to be "taught" how to take milk from his mother; he possesses an instinctual knowledge to open his mouth for feeding. Though we don't know exactly how genes control instincts, it is understood that there is some important connection.

Nurture: Our Social Upbringing

Our genes do contribute to our behavior in other ways, but not as directly as they do to our physiology or our instincts. The reason for this is because our social upbringing also has a strong effect on our personal development.

How we are raised, and how we are taught certain values from our parents and from society in general, can be described as our "nurture." The information we gather on how to behave and how to communicate is not directly encoded in our genes; it must be learned, particularly during childhood. A few things, like what language we will first speak, what political opinions we will hold, or what religion we will follow, are based entirely on our social environment.

Our social environment consists of more than just the parents who nurture us; it also includes our siblings, neighbors, peers, teachers, and anyone around us who may influence our behavior. Even the general society we grow up in has an effect on who we become.

Nature or Nurture: Which Is More Important?

Since both nature and nurture are important, it is hard to know which factor is more influential on a person's character. Sometimes the effect of a person's genes on behavior and personality can be subtle—the person also needs to grow up in the right environment for the effect of the genes to be noticeable. Untangling the web of influences can be difficult, especially since most individuals are raised by the same parents who gave them their genes. Most psychologists now believe that behavioral traits have a basis in both an individual's genes and environment.

What happens when a child is adopted at a young age? Will she turn out to be more like the mother who raises her, or the one who gave birth to her? Well, we can say for certain that the child will have some physical resemblance to her biological mother and that she will speak the same language as her adoptive mother. But her personality will probably contain a unique mix of influences: it may reflect certain tendencies in her genes that were brought out by her social surroundings.

So, we might ask, can we predict what a child will become if we know a lot about the parents who gave the child their genes and raised him or her? If a child has two doctors for parents, will she become a doctor herself? Would the son of two musicians be musically inclined? Maybe. But we can't predict these things for certain because of the complexities of an individual's genes and the wide range of social influences on a child's behavior. Even identical twins who grow up in the same family and attend the same schools will still develop differences in their personalities!

Although our genes and social environment help shape who we become, it is important to remember that they do not predetermine that we will end up a certain way. With strong willpower and self-determination, a person can achieve success. Even someone born with a physical disability or raised in an unhealthy environment will have opportunities to make the most out of life.

Emotions

Emotions can be powerful forces in our behavior. As we develop an awareness of what they are and why we experience them at certain times, we may better understand how to adapt our behavior to feel more of the positive emotions and fewer of the negative ones.

Emotions are complex mental responses to feelings, perceptions, and beliefs. They often result from the processing and interpretation of information that is received from our physical senses—sight, touch, hearing, smell, taste, and pain. Emotions arise without conscious effort and usually include physiological changes.

The ability to experience some of the most common emotions is part of human nature. These emotions include fear, anger, happiness,

sadness, and disgust. Most anthropologists and psychologists believe that people in every part of the world are capable of experiencing these primary emotions in themselves and of recognizing their expression in others. In fact, most mammals express fear and anger in similar, recognizable ways.

The mental states that we experience in emotions are often accompanied by physical symptoms. For example, when we experience fear, our bodies produce a hormone that helps us decide how to react to the situation that is making us feel afraid. Without conscious effort, we also usually display our emotions in facial expressions. Smiling is not something we "learn" how to do; it's a natural reaction to feeling happy!

Often a particular order of events takes place when an emotion is formed. For example, let's say that you are walking in the woods and spot a bear. As your heart beats faster because of the hormone (adrenaline) that is released, you also realize that bears are dangerous. Thus, you feel fear. Finally, you make a decision how to make yourself safe from harm—either by running away or by protecting yourself. Since emotions take place without conscious effort, all of this might happen in less than a second!

Emotional Development

We can learn a great deal about the nature of emotions by studying the emotional level of infants. Many psychologists believe that newborns experience emotional states only in a very general way. They may experience general excitability, or general distress in response to physical sensations such as hunger, pain or warmth. However, they do not experience emotions in the same way as adults, because they do not have a conscious understanding of emotions and their causes.

The fact of the matter is that infants have relatively little capacity for any of the strong emotions that we experience as adults. They experience relatively little fear. It is unclear whether or not they experience love, even though they have an instinctive attraction to their primary caregiver. It is unlikely that they experience anger or rage, even when they are emitting shrill cries of protest from their cribs.

All of these stronger emotions we now believe are learned during the earliest phases of our social development. Fear of a particular

stimulus is often acquired through learning. If you were to be so reckless as to put a rattlesnake into the crib with a young infant, you would find that few if any of the infants displayed any fear. Infants do not know very much about what is dangerous to them. In the beginning, they may have no clear notion of danger or harm at all. As a result, they can observe things that are quite terrifying to many adults and experience no emotional reaction at all.

The ability to experience emotions is part of our nature, or genes. It is also in everyone's nature to express the most common emotions in very similar facial expressions and physical reactions. We all experience anger, for example, in much the same way: our blood pressure rises and our muscles tense up, making our eyes appear squinty.

How we use our minds to interpret information from our senses has a lot to do with our nurture, or how we were raised. Using our understanding of our past experiences, we come to recognize what things make us feel a certain way. For example, one person may learn to fear dogs because he was bit by one as a child; another person may learn to love dogs because she grew up with them. Likewise, a young child does not need to learn how to stomp her feet or pout when she gets mad; what she may learn is that being told she may not have a cookie is a reason to throw a tantrum! The ability to feel angry is part of everyone's nature, but the girl's own angry reaction to her mother's "no!" is part of how she was nurtured.

Learning from Our Emotions

Many emotions may aptly be described as sensory indicators for our mental states. Just as loud noises or sharp pains may warn us about dangers in our physical environment, emotions provide us with another level by which we view and learn about our situations and our relations with others around us. Thus, emotions convey important information to us, and it is important that we deal with this information.

Because emotions are often complex, it can sometimes be very difficult to fully understand where a certain emotion comes from and how to respond to the situation that provoked it. But, to be a healthy and well-balanced person, it is important to try to understand your emotions and how to express them constructively, rather than to ignore or repress them.

Motives

Before we can hope to change our behavior to patterns that can be more effective in getting what we want in life, it is important for us to know why we do the things we do—and just as importantly, why other people do what they do. Sometimes the actions of others seem totally illogical or irrational to us. However, upon closer examination we may discover that their view of the world is significantly different than ours, and that within their view what they attempt to do may make considerably more sense. Their view may seem distorted and inaccurate to us, but they must still respond to it, since it is the only view they have to work with.

Psychologists have determined that there are a wide variety of factors that motivate human behavior, and, moreover, there is generally a hierarchy to these factors. In other words, some basic needs and motives are more fundamental or more important to us than others. Until these fundamental needs are satisfied, we tend to direct most of our energy in their direction. It is only once the basics have been met that we turn our attention to satisfying needs that are higher up the ladder.

Maslow's Hierarchy of Human Needs

MASLOW'S HIERARCHY OF NEEDS

Psychologist Abraham Maslow is best known for identifying a fundamental hierarchy of human needs. Psychologists today disagree about some of his terms or their specific applications, but the existence of a general hierarchy is widely accepted. At the bottom of the hierarchy are the most basic and fundamental needs, the ones that get our top priority if they are ever shaken. The most essential of our needs are simple physical requirements. These include food, drink, shelter, and warmth. A person who is stranded in the desert makes a top priority of finding water and escaping the heat. In such a condition, one stops worrying about such things as personal appearance, what someone else will think of them, or whether or not they are meeting their goals in life. When life itself is threatened, this becomes our number-one priority.

Next up the ladder are broader safety issues. Even when we have the basics of food and shelter, if we feel that we are in danger for any other reason then this becomes our next priority. During times of warfare or violence, people worry about safety. We also worry about safety in unfamiliar situations, such as when we are alone late at night or passing through a dangerous neighborhood. Needs for safety may also apply to financial issues. A person who is afraid of losing their home because they can't meet their mortgage payments may feel threatened. Thus, while safety refers mainly to physical well-being, it may extend to financial security as well.

Once these physiological and safety needs have been met, the next highest priority is what Maslow refers to as belongingness and love—our social needs. We seek to be accepted by others, to be liked by others and to be needed and loved by them. This need is fairly self-explanatory. Given its position on the ladder, it tends to become somewhat less important when either our physical health or our safety is challenged.

Once we have achieved love and belongingness, the next highest level of need involves esteem. We want not only to be loved, but to be respected and admired. We seek praise, recognition, and achievement. We would like to be leaders. We would like to have influence over others. We would like to feel good about ourselves and our personal accomplishments. However, once again, if anything below on the ladder comes loose in our lives, we may delay the pursuit of esteem until we have managed to look after the more fundamental issues.

At the top of Maslow's hierarchy are what he calls self-actualization needs. We may set various intellectual or aesthetic goals for ourselves. We may wish to become more creative. We may wish to pursue a special talent. We may want to stand out as individuals and achieve a unique personal identity. We may have spiritual goals for ourselves. We may be working on self-improvement. This is the highest level at which humans are motivated to achieve their needs and wishes. People are successful at staying at this level only if all the lower-level needs have been adequately fulfilled in their lives.

How Emotional Needs Affect Viewpoints and Motives

Maslow's hierarchy of needs may seem like a very theoretical and academic approach. On the surface, it may not appear to be relevant to our lives. However, consider the following practical example: You are part of a union that is voting on a new contract. The vote is likely to be very close and there is considerable disagreement among the

workers about whether or not to accept management's latest offer. You believe that the offer is not adequate—in fact, you think it is an insult to the workforce. You are prepared to go on strike. You do not understand why so many of your coworkers are hesitant about doing this and seem to want to settle at any cost.

However, let's examine your situation a little more closely and compare it with those of your fellow workers. Perhaps you come from a two-income family. Your spouse may have an adequate income that will help tide you over through a strike. You may have relatively few debts—little or no mortgage, no children going to expensive schools, and no hefty car payments. But some of your coworkers may be considerably more worried about these things. They may fear for their basic physical or safety needs, if the contract should be rejected and the workers are forced to strike.

The difference in viewpoint on this issue corresponds to how far you and your coworkers have each climbed Maslow's hierarchy of needs. With your physical and safety needs looked after, and likely belongingness and love, you are now concerned about self-esteem. You want to receive what you feel you deserve. You want recognition from management. You want to be treated with respect, and you feel that this offer fails to do this. Your decision to reject the contract may be logical. However, another worker's decision to accept it may also be logical if that worker wants to protect his physical well-being or basic economic security.

Here's another example of how differences in emotional needs can affect viewpoints and behavior. Two female friends disagree and have an argument because one of them is involved in a relationship with an abusive male. The person in the abusive relationship is reluctant to end it and unwilling to look at the situation objectively, naïvely hoping for improvement. Her friend, on the other hand, insists that she herself would never tolerate a situation in which someone was taking advantage of her or subjecting her to any form of abuse.

The difference in the two outlooks may once again have to do with Maslow's hierarchy. The person who is stronger willed and more ready to step away from a bad relationship may have achieved a good level of belongingness and love in other aspects of her life. Feeling secure that she is loved, she is able to proceed to the issue of esteem and will

reject any relationship that hurts her self-esteem. However, her friend may not fundamentally feel that she belongs to anyone or that she is loved. She may be so desperate to fulfill this need that she accepts this relationship even though it is less than totally satisfactory.

Once again, the hierarchy of emotional needs helps to color the two women's outlooks and attitudes. Perhaps at some future stage in her development, the woman who is presently at the lower level may make progress in feeling loved to the point where she is no longer tolerant of any form of abuse. At that time, she would have the strength to break off the relationship, even if it means going without a partner for a time until she finds a better situation.

Freud's Theories on the Human Mind

Another complicating factor concerning human motivations is that they often spring from parts of our mind of which we are not fully aware. One of the most important contributions that Sigmund Freud made to the field of psychology was defining different levels of the human mind. Although Freud's theories are not always accepted these days, it is nevertheless useful to examine some of his basic notions. They provide one interesting model of how the mind might work and they help explain why we may find it so difficult to understand our own thought processes.

Freud identified two basic parts of the mind, which he called the conscious and the unconscious. The conscious mind involves the thoughts of which we are readily aware. When we are thinking to ourselves about what we want to do in a given situation, we are using our conscious mind. However, we also have an unconscious mind which is active "behind the scenes"—and we do not always know what is going on there. Sometimes dreams can provide clues to motives or anxieties that are being dealt with by our unconscious minds. According to Freud, much motivation comes from the unconscious mind, which means that it can be very difficult to be fully aware of specific motives in a given situation.

Freud gave the term "ego" to the conscious part of the mind. The ego is the part of the mind that makes deliberate decisions. It is aware of sensory data and our train of thought. When you make a decision

about what to eat in a restaurant, or whether to make a left or right turn at a traffic light, your ego is at work.

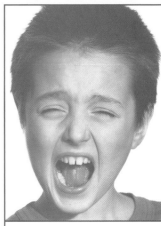

Freud divided the unconscious mind into two elements that he called the "id" and the "superego." The id is the part of the mind that tries to achieve pleasure in life. It is where our fundamental wants and drives originate. If we compare the ego to the driver of a car, the id is a child in the back seat screaming, "I want this," or constantly making restless complaints or protests about being bored or hungry. In other words, the id is the part of the unconscious mind that can get us into trouble. The ego must control the id and its desires or we will tend to wander into behaviors that are not always socially acceptable.

The superego, on the other hand, is what we often think of as "conscience." It is the part of us that realizes we cannot always do what we want the moment that we want to do it. It is aware that there are such things as right and wrong, that we have social obligations, and that we have to consider the feelings and well-being of others. The superego is the part of the mind that is concerned with morals and ethics. When the ego is being driven too much by the id, the superego interjects doubts or a feeling of guilt or remorse in an attempt to steer us back onto a better path.

The Preconscious Mind

Some psychologists make a further distinction to identify what they call the preconscious mind. The preconscious mind exists just slightly below the level of the conscious mind or the ego. It holds ideas or motives that are very close to our direct thought processes, including memories. By stopping and thinking a bit, we can generally get in touch with the wishes and ideas of our preconscious mind.

Psychoanalytic Therapy

However, most psychologists believe that other motives and ideas are buried much deeper in our unconscious mind, far below the level of the preconscious. One of the purposes of psychoanalytic therapy, a form of counseling with a psychologist, is to try to access some of what is buried deep down in the subconscious. Sometimes strategies such as hypnosis are used to help unlock the deeper levels of the subconscious. The assumption is that what is buried far below the surface of our minds is of considerable importance to understanding our motives and reactions, and those levels are worth getting at and exploring.

Many psychologists think of the complete mind as being much like an iceberg floating in the sea. Only the tip of an iceberg sticks up above the water; the bulk of it is actually below the surface. The ego is the part of our mind that is above the surface. However, the larger and more complex areas of the superego and id are buried deeper down.

It is little wonder we sometimes surprise and confuse ourselves with the way we react to certain situations or with strong emotional responses that catch us unprepared. This is also why the process of self-knowledge, which is discussed in greater detail later in this text, is so fundamentally important if we are to gain self-control. There is so much of our minds "under the water" that we need to do some exploration if we are truly going to know and understand ourselves.

Defense Mechanisms

Ideally, before we make any decisions in life we would take time out to study the situation and to probe our own needs, ideas, and motives at every level of our mind before coming to the best possible conclusion. In the real world, however, we often have difficulty doing this. Sometimes, immediate decisions or responses are required. We are forced to take action in social situations before we have had a chance to figure out how we feel about the situation, what outcome we would like to see, or what the best means might be in order to achieve it.

When our mental circuits get overloaded we often resort to defense mechanisms as a way of dealing with or avoiding situations that are unpleasant or causing us stress and anxiety. Sometimes defense mechanisms can be a good thing because they can bring us immediate and temporary relief from a stressful situation that is overpowering at that moment. However, if we rely on defense mechanisms and use them as a crutch, we never get to the root of our problems, which invariably tend to get worse. Thus, it is important to understand when we are using defense mechanisms so that we can decide to limit their use and replace them with more positive and thought-out reactions and responses.

Procrastination and Repression

One basic defense mechanism is simply to ignore a situation. Procrastination can be a defense mechanism. We don't know quite what to do, so we do nothing. We make plans to do something later,

perhaps with the hope that we will no longer have to do the unpleasant task by the time "later" comes.

A more severe form of this defense mechanism is repression. When we repress something we push it down into our unconscious mind where we will not have to be aware of it and where we will find it less painful. For example, feelings of hostility are often repressed.

When we repress something, we are not just putting it off. We begin to deny its existence, and this is seldom a healthy thing to do. Sometimes repression goes to an extreme form and becomes amnesia. When amnesia occurs we lose all memory of a situation and any of the details surrounding it. Serious traumatic incidents, as well as injuries to the brain, can bring on amnesia, which may be either temporary or permanent.

Rationalization

Another extremely common defense mechanism is what is known as rationalization. Rationalization means that we cannot face the real reason for our behavior, so we invent other reasons and try to convince ourselves that they are correct. A common form of rationalization is blaming others or making excuses about why we cannot do something. For example, if we forget to do something important that our boss or someone else in authority asked us to do, we may begin to lie about how busy we were with other things and how impossible it was to do what was requested of us. Those other things may only have taken a small amount of our day, but we exaggerate them in order to make an excuse.

The problem is that we don't always just lie to other people with rationalizations; we actually lie to ourselves. We convince ourselves that there is a good reason not to do something or a good reason not to try to achieve something simply because we do not want to face up to the task of how to go about doing it. Another form of rationalization is when we try to convince ourselves that something we failed to achieve was not worth achieving in the first place.

If we tried and failed at something, we may tell ourselves that the thing we strived for wasn't important or wouldn't have been useful. If we lose an important relationship with a loved one, possibly through our own fault, we may try to convince ourselves that the other person

was not suitable for us or wasn't a very good friend or lover, and we are better off without them.

Regression

Another form of defense mechanism is what is known as regression. Regression tends to occur when we begin to make some improvements in our life, but then become confused or stressed, or don't see the results we wanted immediately. This causes us to lapse back into our old behaviors. People who try to give up use of harmful or addictive substances experience a regression when they lapse back into bad habits. A person who goes on a diet to lose weight but gives up after a couple of weeks is regressing to former behaviors.

Sometimes we regress by resorting to behaviors that are associated with earlier stages of our lives. Suddenly, we may begin acting like teenagers or children again, sulking, throwing tantrums, demanding attention, or doing unproductive things to retaliate when we feel that someone has wronged us.

Denial

A final form of defense mechanism worth considering here is denial. In denial, we are so insecure about a situation that we simply pretend that it does not exist. This is similar to amnesia, except in this case there are no gaps in our memory. We are simply refusing to admit reality. For example, a woman who is being frequently assaulted by her husband is clearly a victim of an abusive domestic relationship. However, she may be so overwhelmed with confusion as to what to do about the situation that she denies that her husband is actually abusive. To others, she may claim that her bruises are the result of accidents. She may also try to convince herself that she was the one who was in the wrong. She exonerates her husband's bad behavior because she does not know what to do about it. She has resorted to the defense mechanism of denial to keep from being overwhelmed with fear and anxiety about the situation.

Defense mechanisms are usually unhealthy ways of dealing with situations. They never get to the root of our problems, so the prospect for improvement is very slim. The best way to overcome reliance on defense mechanisms is to accept the fact that we are using them and that they are not constructive elements in our lives.

Summary

To build effective relationships with other people, it is important that you understand the foundations of human behavior. This includes how genetics, environmental factors, and free will shape a person's personality, development, and instincts. Both genetics and social upbringing help shape who we become and what we are good at doing, but they do not predetermine that we will end up a certain way. With strong willpower and self-determination, a person can achieve success.

Sometimes your colleagues, clients, friends, or family members may behave in ways that seem illogical or irrational to you. For this reason, it is helpful to understand human emotions and what motivates people to react and behave as they do. How a person responds to a given situation often depends on how well their emotional needs are being met at that time. Emotional needs are hierarchical in nature. It is only when basic needs for food, shelter, water, and safety are met that people can focus on higher-level needs, such as social needs and self-esteem. Safety needs include not only physical safety, but also financial security.

Finally, at your workplace and in your daily life, you will sometimes encounter people who are so overwhelmed by a personal problem that they will deny that it even exists in order to avoid dealing with it. Knowing about the defense mechanisms people use to deal with or avoid stressful situations will be helpful to you in these cases.

Key Terms

Term	Definition
Conscious mind	The conscious mind contains the thoughts that we are actively aware of.
Defense mechanisms	Defense mechanisms are psychological strategies used by people to protect themselves against stress and anxiety or situations with which they feel unable to cope.
Denial	Denial is a defense mechanism that involves pretending that a difficult situation or problem does not exist.
Genes	All living things, including humans, contain a complete set of special molecules called genes within the nucleus of each of their living cells. Genes control many individual traits and features, including our size, shape, gender, skin color, and brain development.
Ego	The ego is the part of the conscious mind that makes deliberate decisions and is aware of sensory data and our train of thought.
Genetics	Genetics is the science of heredity and variation in living organisms.
Id	The id is the part of the unconscious mind that tries to achieve pleasure in life. The ego must control the id and its desires if we are to avoid socially unacceptable behavior.
Maslow's hierarchy of human needs	This is a theory proposed by psychologist Abraham Maslow that states that human needs are hierarchical in nature. Only when basic physiological needs are met can a person focus on meeting higher needs, such as social needs and self-esteem.
Motives	A motive is an emotional need or desire that causes a person to act in a certain way.
Preconscious mind	Believed to be lying between the conscious and unconscious mind, the preconscious holds ideas or motives that are very close to our direct thought processes, including unrepressed memories.

Key Terms

Term	Definition
Procrastination	Procrastination is a defense mechanism that involves putting off a task or a decision until later.
Psychoanalytic therapy	Also called psychoanalysis, psychoanalytic therapy sometimes involves the use of hypnosis and other techniques to access and analyze unconscious mental processes.
Rationalization	Rationalization involves inventing what we believe to be a logical justification for a belief, decision, or action, when we cannot face the real reason.
Regression	Regression involves returning to an earlier thought or behavior pattern to avoid emotional stress or anxiety.
Repression	Repression is a defense mechanism that involves placing uncomfortable thoughts in a relatively inaccessible area of our unconscious mind.
Self-actualization	Self-actualization is the human need to make the most of one's abilities and to strive to be the best that one can. In Maslow's hierarchy of needs, self-actualization is the final stage of psychological development.
Superego	The superego is the part of the mind concerned with morals, ethics, and social obligations. It functions as a person's "conscience."
Unconscious mind	Also called the subconscious mind, the unconscious is the part of the mind that a person is not actively aware of. According to Freud, the unconscious is hidden but has a very large effect on human behavior.

CHAPTER 3

The Process of Socialization

Highlights of the Chapter

This Chapter Covers:

- The social development of children

- Developmental factors that may lead to social maladjustment

- The role that culture and social institutions play in the process of socialization

Introduction

To some the word "socialization" may sound like something one does to become popular. Actually, that definition would not be totally wrong. To social scientists socialization is a general term for the process we go through in learning how to participate with others in our society.

This chapter describes the social development process, which begins when we are young children and continues throughout our lives as we adjust to cultural expectations in social institutions, the workplace, and broader society. This chapter also discusses the role that culture and social institutions play in the socialization process and the developmental factors that can lead to social maladjustment.

Culture

What we need to learn in order to become socialized can loosely be defined as culture. Many people think of culture as art, music, and literature. These are portions of our culture, but the term covers a much broader range. Our culture also includes radio, television, newspapers, magazines, and the Internet. It encompasses our political traditions, and civic and religious holidays and rituals. It may include

elements of how we work, dress, shop, drive our cars, spend our vacations, and even how we speak and greet one another. Any knowledge or behavior that others in our society expect from us can be considered part of our culture.

Through socialization, which begins before we are even old enough to talk, we come to learn our culture and its values and norms. The many people and institutions who guide this process are called agents. These include our parents, schools, peer groups, religious institutions, the mass media, and many others.

Social Expectations

The important thing about culture is that it is linked to social expectations. When these are wantonly disregarded, we can anticipate consequences or penalties. Culture is part of what makes us comfortable in society, and when someone attacks it or belittles it, they are apt to get a negative reaction from those around them.

There are some elements of culture that are common to almost all of humanity. However, many if not most cultural elements vary significantly from one part of the world to another. In some cultures, a handshake is a common greeting. In others, the same gesture is accomplished with a bow or a kiss on the cheek. Some cultures permit women to be nude or topless on public beaches, while others would arrest them for such behavior. Places or creatures may be sacred to one religious group and have no meaning to another. Even minor details, such as which side of the road you drive your car on, tend to vary significantly.

As we study how human beings adapt and relate to the people around them, the importance of culture cannot be overlooked. Culture is more than an accumulation of habits. It reflects the goals, values, and beliefs of a people. This is why it is taken seriously in a society. Most people do not regard their culture as a bunch of dumb rules. They see it is a tradition that links them to their ancestors and that preserves and protects the quality and value of their lives.

Culture and Freedom of Expression

As human beings develop, there is inevitably some clash between the dictates of the culture and a person's desire to assert an individual

identity. Some cultures are very rigid and permit little individual expression. Most of us consider ourselves fortunate to be living in North America, where individual freedom is actually seen as an important part of our culture, rather than as a challenge to it. Still, even in a relatively liberal and permissive society, most people feel the need for the secure boundaries a culture provides. There are limits to the tolerance of unusual behaviors, especially ones which appear to threaten cultural values.

Whatever opinion one may have of this reaction in people, it is important to accept that it is a logical and predictable one. If the staunch individualist is ignorant about the culture and its significance to others, he or she is likely to encounter opposition and even hostility. How many Hollywood movies have been made over the years in which a person from a Western culture visits a faraway tribe, begins carelessly touching or damaging some sacred object, and soon finds himself lashed to a stake or stewing in a pot? Those plots often involve an exaggeration or caricature of cultural imperatives. Nonetheless, in real life, people often find themselves in a less literal form of hot water when they deliberately or accidentally violate some element of culture.

Adjusting to Workplace Culture

One interesting point about culture is that it exists not only on the level of races or nations, but within much smaller groups and organizations. For example, a specific company where you may find yourself working will have a distinct culture. The culture may include things such as a formal or informal dress code, habits about how and where breaks or meals are taken, or customs concerning use of parking spaces. There may even be unwritten guidelines about behaviors, such as whether one employee is or is not expected to greet another employee whom they pass by in the office or the store.

On this smaller scale, just as on the larger one, a person who is unfamiliar with the local culture may end up violating it in a way that makes them stand out. This behavior may make others feel hurt, resentful, or critical of the nonstandard behaviors. Whenever you enter a new social environment, just as when you enter a new country, it is important to be extra sensitive and observant about cultural issues. Most successful people deal with cultural uncertainty by being

temporarily less assertive or outgoing, following the lead of others, and making friendly gestures that indicate their desire to learn the rules and fit in.

Social Institutions

Institutions within society are important shapers of our culture. The main institutions are the government, organized religions, the mass media, the educational system and large social organizations. Major charities also play a role in shaping our culture, as do organized leagues for sporting events.

In parts of the country where there is one large and dominant employer, that corporation is also a primary social institution. This may apply to a mining town, a farming cooperative, or a major manufacturing plant.

Social institutions are not only important in originating culture and social expectations, but they are also important agents of the socialization process itself. Our institutions create our schools, daycares, cultural events, and entertainment outlets, and they provide the settings for many of our everyday social interactions.

Social institutions shape our society as a whole. Some grow in size, power, and security by influencing others to join them, accept them, or support them in some way. A key example is a political party. Most parties support specific goals and ideologies that can be achieved only if they are able to persuade a majority of citizens to vote for them. In a more indirect way, religious groups sometimes compete for public support, especially with regard to key issues that may be disputed or are of a controversial nature, such as abortion.

Social institutions influence our behavior and our thinking in many ways. Sometimes they do so openly through direct campaigning. Advertising is a means of attempting to influence the opinions and behaviors of others. It is often used to convince consumers to buy a product. Ads are also used to promote candidates, causes, philosophies, patriotism, or cultural events.

We have been so continuously bombarded by the influences of social institutions throughout our lives that we often do not fully appreciate

how important they have been in the shaping of our habits and opinions. It is often difficult to determine which thoughts and opinions are truly our own—ones that we have arrived at through experience or reflection—and those that we have acquired passively and perhaps uncritically from groups within our society.

Sometimes on the news we see people in other parts of the world behaving in ways that seem irrational to us, whether they be acts of war, persecution, racism, or other forms of aggression or destruction. What we often fail to realize is that these people have been brought up in a different cultural environment from us and have been directly influenced by some very different social institutions.

Religious and Political Beliefs

Some social institutions, such as organized religions, are formed in response to belief systems.

These beliefs touch on fundamental issues, such as the following:

- The existence or nature of God

- Codes of moral conduct

- Views on the role of government in society and the need to help others

- Individual rights and freedoms

Because there are deep fundamental differences among human beings on these issues, religious and government institutions vary greatly—not only from one nation to another, but even within a single culture.

The topic of religious beliefs and institutions is too complex to be discussed here. However, it is useful to take a brief look at some of the world's major political ideologies in order to appreciate their impact on society and the process of socialization.

Left-wing, Right-wing, or Centrist?

You may have heard politicians or political parties described as "left-wing" or "right-wing." These terms refer to basic views of the role of

government in our society. The right wing of the political spectrum emphasizes personal freedom and the right to personal property and wealth. This view states that government should be kept as small as possible, handling only the basic necessities of society, such as national defense, and interfering in the lives of citizens as little as possible. Right-wing individuals generally feel that governments have grown too large these days, and they tend to support lower taxes.

The left-wing or liberal side of the political spectrum has a very different viewpoint. Left-wing individuals believe that in a society of minimal government, great inequalities tend to develop between the rich and the poor, or the privileged and the disadvantaged. They believe it is important for government to level out this playing field somewhat, to help the poor, to ensure equal opportunities, and to increase taxes on the wealthy as a means of redistributing some of society's wealth.

Many people fall into a category that has been described as centrist, or middle of the road. They agree with some of what the left-wing parties assert, but tend to side with the right wing on other issues. They wish to avoid the extremists at either end of the spectrum. In a given election, they may be swayed toward one side or the other, and they often make the critical difference in the outcome.

In the United States, the Republican Party is generally regarded as more right-wing or conservative than the Democratic Party. In Canada, the Conservative Party is generally seen as being right of center, with the Liberal Party situated left of center and the New Democratic Party farther to the left.

Extremism

Extremism is a term used to describe the actions or ideologies of individuals or groups outside the perceived political center of a society. Socialist or communist parties are viewed as being left-wing extremists. They advocate strict government regulation of most aspects of society, sometimes even at the expense of personal freedoms.

Increasingly, we are also seeing the emergence of extreme right-wing groups. Examples include some of the private militias that have been gaining popularity in parts of rural North America. Some of these groups are so concerned about government interference in their lives that they advocate overthrowing the government by means of armed force.

The rest of the world is similarly divided in terms of political ideologies. This is one of the major causes of strife, aggression, and warfare. However, within a society, these political parties and institutions also play an important role in shaping the process of socialization and in defining expectations for behavior. The successful political groups are the ones that acquire the power to pass laws that make belief systems both formal and enforceable. Failure to conform to behavioral expectations at this level can result in imprisonment or even execution.

Social Development

The first and most important agent of socialization for developing human beings is the family. Psychologists tell us that the most important and enduring aspects of our personalities develop during the early years before we are old enough to go off to school. During this period of time, our parents, siblings, and extended family members largely are our society.

We learn about the world mainly by observing these individuals. If their outlooks and behaviors are typical of the rest of society, then it is relatively straightforward to make the progression from family life into the larger society as we progress through childhood. However, if family values or behaviors are radically at odds with those of society, we may have difficulty understanding, accepting, and overcoming these early influences. For example, if we are exposed to violence in the home, it may be hard to understand and adjust to the fact that the rest of society does not consider this behavior acceptable. We may become insecure, uneasy, or develop a negative self-image if we begin to believe that what we have learned through early socialization is unreliable or unacceptable.

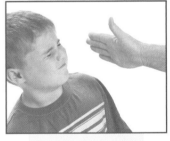

In chapter 2, we looked at the issue of nature versus nurture. We examined the role that instinct seems to play in the earliest stages of human development. During the first year of life we experience rapid growth. Our priority is the physical development of what are known as sensory and motor (physical-movement) skills. This part of our development is triggered by instinct and at first is largely independent of the observations of other persons. As such, it tends to follow a very predictable timetable in most babies who are free of illnesses or other physical limitations.

The vast majority of infants become capable of holding their head erect and steady at around the age of three months. Visual capabilities develop in a complex pattern over the first six months or so of life. Tests have shown that most two-week-old babies tend to look primarily at the internal features of a face, such as the eyes, rather than respond to an overall shape. Color receptors are not fully functional until babies are about two months old. It is not until the age of three to five months that babies become adept at merging the visual images of both eyes into true stereoscopic vision.

The Socialization Process in Children

The importance of "nurture" can be seen in the fact that children are not quite so predictable in the development of social and personal skills, such as learning to talk, play with others, and use the toilet. To a large extent, the socialization of toddlers and young children varies in proportion to the quantity and quality of stimulation that they receive.

However, this is true only to a point. The socialization process is still largely driven from within. Even children with comparatively absent or neglectful parents make concerted and remarkable efforts to learn about the world around them as quickly as they can. For example, the basic process of learning a mother tongue is accomplished with an impressive efficiency adults find hard to replicate if they try to learn a second language later in life.

Besides the frequency of contact and stimulation, another reason why parents are so influential in the development of children's early social awareness is that parents make deliberate attempts to influence their child's socialization. Although children are born with certain instincts, parents develop instinctive responses towards their children as well. As throughout the animal kingdom, human parents have a strong instinctive urge to protect their children.

In our complex human lifestyles, this protection extends well beyond prevention of accidents and elimination of physical dangers. Parents have learned through experience how important the socialization process is to a person's well-being and happiness throughout life. They have observed that people experience varying rates of success within society, and that some degree of deprivation or suffering is associated

with socialization failures. Therefore, they try to protect their children from this form of harm by deliberately teaching their children the values, customs, and skills that they will need in order to participate in society.

As the child grows older, portions of this fundamental parental responsibility are delegated or passed on to various social institutions, including schools, churches, and organized social groups. At some point along the way, the significance of the family as the primary agent of socialization begins to diminish. Instead, the child becomes increasingly influenced by his or her peer group and by the larger society, as perceived through direct experience and through the media. This is also a critical part of social development because it leads gradually towards independence, which is necessary in order for a person to function in the adult world.

The transitions are gradual and often confusing. Parents are often unsure when they should back away and exert less direct control over their children. Children, in their natural drive towards independence and adulthood, may try to pull away too soon, or they may rebel against the control of parents and social institutions.

Social Maladjustment

When all goes well, the development process leads along a steady, if sometimes bumpy, road toward eventual independence as a reasonably happy and effective member of adult society. However, any number of factors can short-circuit this process and lead to developmental problems.

Problems in social development may result from many causes, including genetic disorders, injuries or illness. They can also result from abnormalities or deficiencies in a child's environment. Abuse, isolation, understimulation, inconsistency, and deprivation may all be factors. Parents may fail to be effective in helping the socialization process of their children due to the effects of poverty, physical or mental illness, or gaps in their own socialization as children or adults.

Social maladjustment can lead to problems such as deviance, alienation, and aggression. Deviance can be loosely defined as abnormal and unacceptable behavior that is considered harmful.

Alienation is a process in which children become separated from the mainstream of society or from their peer group. It is often accompanied by feelings of inadequacy, frustration, or depression. Aggression is hostile, injurious, or destructive behavior meant to cause harm or pain. It can be either physical or verbal. Aggression often results when fundamental needs are not being adequately met and the child blames others for this deprivation.

An excessive concern for maladjustment's root causes, such as an unhealthy social environment, may often appear to diminish the element of free will in human behavior and choices. An extreme form of this perspective can make us all seem like puppets, doomed by deficiencies in our upbringing to act out roles over which we have little true understanding or control.

Very few people today accept that restrictive view of what human beings are all about. We are influenced by both nature and nurture, but neither controls us or dictates what we must become. These factors may create habits, tendencies, weaknesses, and blind spots, but they do not reduce us to puppets.

Sooner or later, we all get the chance to observe and study a wide range of human behavior in the world at large, beyond the narrow influences of our particular upbringing. We get the chance to make rational choices, and even to change fundamental aspects of our outlooks and personalities. However, that change is not always as easy to accomplish as we might expect. It is made more difficult when we don't understand the influences of our past, which may tend to steer us back toward some unwanted habits.

Summary

Socialization is the process we go through in learning how to participate with others in our society. The traditions, norms, and attitudes we need to understand in order to become socialized can loosely be defined as culture. Any knowledge or behavior that others in our society expect from us can be considered part of our culture.

Culture exists not only on the level of races or nations, but also within smaller organizations, such as social groups and the workplace. It is linked to social expectations. People who violate cultural norms often draw a negative reaction.

Through socialization, which begins before we are even old enough to talk, we come to learn our culture and its values and norms. The agents who guide this process include our parents, schools, peer groups, religious institutions, and the mass media. For young children, the most important agent of socialization is the family. Later, as a child grows older, some responsibility for socialization is shifted to social institutions, including schools, churches, and organized social groups.

Social maladjustment or problems in social development may result from many causes, including genetic disorders, injuries or illness, or abnormalities or deficiencies in a child's environment. Maladjustment can lead to problems such as deviance, alienation, and aggression.

Term	Definition
Advertising	Advertising is a means of attempting to influence the opinions and behaviors of others. It is often used to convince consumers to buy a product.
Aggression	Aggression is hostile, injurious, or destructive behavior meant to cause harm or pain. It can be either physical or verbal.
Alienation	Alienation is a process by which a person becomes separated from the mainstream of society or from his or her peer group.
Centrist	Political centrists support moderate policies that favor the middle ground between political extremes. Centrism lands in the middle between left- and right-wing politics.
Culture	A collection of a society's traditions, norms, and attitudes. Culture includes not only art, music, literature, radio, television, films, and newspapers; it also includes shared traditions, holidays, rituals, and beliefs, plus how we work, dress, shop, greet each other, and speak.
Deviance	Deviance is immoral behavior that is socially unacceptable. Examples include damaging property and stealing.
Extremism	Extremism is a term used to describe the actions or ideologies of individuals or groups far outside the perceived political center of a society.
Left-wing	The left-wing or liberal side of the political spectrum emphasizes the importance of government intervention to level the playing field between rich and poor, by ensuring equal economic opportunities and taxing the wealthy at a higher rate to redistribute some of society's wealth.

Term	Definition
Motor skills	Developed in infancy and early childhood, motor skills involve the use of our muscles in a goal-directed manner. Gross motor skills include lifting one's head, rolling over, sitting up, balancing, crawling, and walking. Fine motor skills include the ability to manipulate small objects, transfer objects from hand to hand, and perform various hand-eye coordination tasks.
Right-wing	The right-wing or conservative side of the political spectrum emphasizes personal freedom, the right to personal property and wealth, minimal government spending and programs, and lower taxes.
Sensory perception	Sensory perception involves the gathering of information through five senses: vision, taste, touch, smell, and hearing. Infants must develop their sense of sight. Children have full visual perception by two years of age.
Socialization	Socialization is a process through which an individual comes to understand his or her own culture and its norms and values. Agents such as families, schools, peer groups, religious institutions, and the mass media help direct this process.
Social institutions	Social institutions shape our society as a whole and originate aspects of culture and social expectations. The main social institutions are the government, organized religions, the mass media, the educational system, and large social organizations.
Social maladjustment	Social maladjustment refers an individual's refusal of society's rules and norms. It may lead to other behavioral problems such as deviance, alienation, and aggression.

CHAPTER 4

Social Issues in General

Highlights of the Chapter

This Chapter Covers:

- Broader social issues that affect society: poverty, alcoholism and drug abuse, domestic violence, and racism and discrimination.

Introduction

In this chapter, we will turn our attention to the broader social issues that affect us as members of society. These include poverty, alcoholism and drug abuse, domestic violence, and racism and discrimination. These are common social issues that may affect our communities, our workplaces, and even our families and personal relationships.

It is important for us to study these greater social issues, because they help shape the world around us. Our world is the stage upon which all of our personal relationships are played out. Understanding these issues can help us appreciate the effects they have on our own lives and those of the people with whom we come into contact.

Poverty

Poverty is more than just a problem in developing nations, where little economic opportunity may exist. It is also a problem here in North America, and it has an effect on all of us in our society, regardless of our personal situations. Here in North America, poverty is sometimes hidden from view. The most serious victims tend to live in inner cities or in remote rural areas. Because we may not live or work in these areas, we may not be aware of the extent of the problem, or the degree of suffering in the most devastated areas.

Sociologists are very much aware of the existence of poverty in American and Canadian societies. Social workers and government officials try to create programs to help those in need. Some of these programs are more effective than others. Public understanding and attitudes are often critical to the success of achieving social goals.

Defining Poverty

There are various definitions of what constitutes living in poverty here in North America. Experts come up with formulas, so that they can quantify the problem and keep track of positive or negative trends. The United States government defines the poverty line by taking the minimal cost of what it would take to feed a person for one year, and then multiplying that amount by three. A person who earns less than that amount is in absolute poverty. For an American who lives alone, the official poverty line is an income slightly more than $10,000 a year. When one-third or more of a family's income is spent on food, and more is spent on clothing and shelter, there will be little money left for such things as healthcare, education, transportation, and recreation. Families in poverty generally find it impossible to save any money, so they have little security for the future. This can create considerable tension and stress within the home environment and lead to a wide range of social problems, ranging from juvenile delinquency to suicide.

Some experts define the poverty line as earning less than half of what the average person earns in a year. This method defines relative poverty. It has more to do with comparing an individual's income and expenses against a group average.

In chapter 3, "The Process of Socialization," we looked at how political viewpoints differ within our society. Poverty is an issue that often tends to form a dividing line of public opinion. Some see poverty as a disgrace for which society as a whole is to blame and which society must act together to address and solve. Others see the plight of the poor as largely their own fault: they blame them for a lack of effort or initiative at solving their own problems.

The Social and Economic Costs of Poverty

Very few experts on social issues share this second point of view. They view poverty as a vicious circle that is very difficult to escape without outside help from society. However, there is a more self-serving,

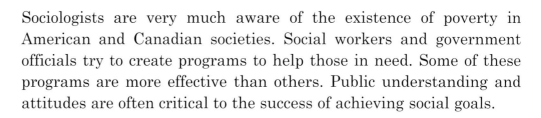

economic reason for society to take an interest in ridding itself of poverty. Social economists are able to demonstrate that victims of poverty cost society considerably more than the money that is distributed to them directly through welfare or unemployment insurance programs.

Poverty is at the core of a broad range of important social problems, including crime, drugs, and prostitution. It fuels the need for expensive services such as health care, shelters, homes and orphanages, prisons, and a broad range of other government programs—all of which cost North American taxpayers billions of dollars a year. This doesn't take into account the extra money that citizens spend privately insuring and arming themselves, and trying to protect themselves from some of the negative repercussions of having to live in a world where a significant portion of the population suffers from serious physical, economic, social, and psychological deprivation and disadvantage. Worse, much of this money is spent coping with the problem without fixing it, so it is money that will have to be spent over and over again.

Alcoholism and Drug Abuse

Like poverty—to which they are often related—alcoholism and drug abuse are personal problems that take their toll on society as a whole. Alcoholism has been a serious problem in North America for decades. It contributes to about 50 percent of all fatal traffic accidents, and a staggering proportion of health care costs. It contributes to many thefts, assaults, and other violent crimes, and it is often the key factor in chronic unemployment and domestic violence.

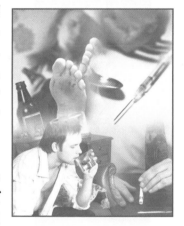

The related problem of drug abuse has been on the rise again in recent years, especially among young people. In some cities, more than half of all high school students claim that they have at least experimented with some illegal drug. The vast majority of students know someone who is a frequent drug user. Drugs are easy to obtain in most American and Canadian high schools. Law enforcement efforts to deal with the problem have had limited success so far.

This is too complex a topic to be dealt with here in more than a passing fashion. However, it is relevant to this text in two ways. First of all, it is an example of the type of complex social problem that sociologists study and that professional social workers and counselors address

daily. Secondly, it is important to understand the impact of alcohol and drugs on the personal human relations issues that we will address in chapters 6 to 10.

Sooner or later alcohol and drugs touch us all, either personally or through a family member or friend. We must all decide what our own philosophy and behavior will be in this area. In times of stress or personal crisis, we may face the temptation of using chemical substances as a short-term "solution" to the pain and unpleasant emotions that we may feel welling up within us.

It is ironic that many of us first become exposed to alcohol and drugs in social settings such as parties. The irony lies in the fact that the long-term effects of chemical abuse lead not only to economic and health consequences, but to antisocial behaviors that can cripple our human relations efforts. Just as there is a vicious cycle to poverty, there is a similar pattern with people who fall victim to substance abuse. It erodes our resources, our relationships and our basic self-esteem. In doing so, it adds to the unpleasant aware nesses and emotions that propelled us to try this escape hatch in the first place.

When Does Substance Use Become a Problem?

It is not always easy to define when a person has a chemical dependency problem—and it is harder still to identify such a problem in ourselves. Alcohol in particular is a legal substance that is used in moderation by many happy and successful people in our society. How do we know when we are slipping over the imaginary line that defines us as a problem drinker?

Many of the warning signs have to do with human relations problems that begin to creep slowly but unmistakably into our lives.

We clearly have a problem if one or more of the following things begin to occur:

- If drinking or drug use contributes directly or indirectly to arguments or problems with bosses, coworkers, friends, spouses, parents, or family members.

- If it causes strain in relationships or makes people back away from us.

- If it causes financial losses or wasted opportunities that detract from our standard of living.

- If it also causes accidents, injuries, illness, or trouble with the law, then the problem is even more serious.

It is difficult to deal successfully with a substance abuse problem without obtaining professional help. Trained counselors understand these problems thoroughly, and they know what help and support is available.

Domestic Violence

Domestic violence has always been an important social issue. We hear more about it today than we did in the past. This is partly due to greater public awareness and discussion of the problem.

Domestic violence includes physical, sexual, or verbal abuse of children by parents or other adults, and violence between spouses. Women and children are most often the victims, although senior citizens and even some men can suffer from such violence as well.

What Constitutes Abuse?

Sexual abuse includes rape, but also fondling and/or unwanted touching. It also includes the use of sexually related threats or humiliation as a way of achieving dominance or control over another person.

Physical abuse includes assaults of all types. It is important to understand that under the law, assault can be physical or verbal. A threat or a gesture that causes one to fear for one's safety is a form of assault and is against the law.

Verbal abuse can be more subtle than a direct assault. Any attempt to break down a person's dignity and will, humiliate them, or destroy their self-confidence and self-esteem are forms of verbal abuse. For example, a parent who tells a child that he is evil, stupid, unlovable or destined to failure is committing a form of verbal abuse. Parents may verbally oppose wrong things that their children do, but when they attack children personally, they are violating their human rights as defined in our society.

It is sometimes difficult to determine what forms of parental discipline may be considered abusive. Even experts don't always agree on this issue. Some approve of corporal punishment, such as spanking, if it is done under control and without causing excessive pain or any physical harm. However, many organizations of doctors and psychologists oppose corporal punishment of any form. In some European countries, it is a criminal act for a parent to strike a child under any circumstance.

It is important to realize that children can also be abusive to their parents, both physically and verbally. Senior citizens may also face abuse at the hands of children or adults, and this is a growing concern as our population gets older.

Like all other social problems, these issues become broader than the individuals who suffer directly from them. There is a larger cost to society as a whole in coping with the repercussions of abuse, which include violent crime, increased drug and alcohol abuse, unemployment, displacement, alienation, and other strains on the education and health care systems. Once again, there is a tendency toward a vicious circle: it has been documented that abused children are more likely than others to become abusive parents—unless something is done to understand and break the cycle. As with other social problems, professional counseling is often critical in accomplishing this.

Racism and Discrimination in Society

We are all aware of the devastating effect that racial discrimination and ethnic conflicts have had on human history. We recognize and understand the meaning of racism in its most flagrant and devastating forms, such as race riots, racially motivated assaults, and civil wars or other conflicts motivated by racial, ethnic, or religious differences. However, we are sometimes not as quick to see the more subtle signs of racism underway within our own society.

What Are Racism and Discrimination?

Racism is the belief that a person's race is at least partially responsible for his or her individual abilities or limitations. Racism could also be the belief that one race is superior to others.

The term discrimination refers generally to unfair treatment on the basis of specific differences among individuals that are related to their background and not to their unique performance or personality. This may mean discrimination based on race, religion, ethnic origin, sex, age, sexual orientation, political viewpoint—or even, in some cases, physical appearance, size, or other superficial traits. A related problem is discrimination based on illness or disability.

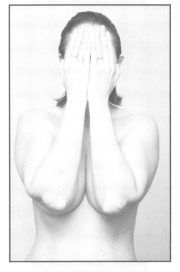

It is important to understand that when we refer to racism and similar forms of discrimination we are talking about acts that by definition are unjust. Discrimination occurs when someone treats a person unfairly because he or she is different, and because that difference provokes unmerited assumptions or fears. In other words, discrimination takes people with faces and makes them faceless. It ignores who they actually are, and reacts to them as two-dimensional stereotypes.

Our society today expects us to give individuals the benefit of the doubt unless or until they have behaved in some objectionable manner. Discrimination is a denial of that opportunity, which is the right of everyone in our country. It is a prejudgment, and the unjustified withdrawal of a chance to participate and to be treated fairly.

It should be emphasized that discrimination does not only pertain to people from other races or other nationalities. Of equal importance in our society today are issues of discrimination against women in certain job settings, or unequal pay given to women. Other examples include discrimination against the elderly or against older workers, discrimination against married people with children in certain apartment buildings, and numerous other such examples. The point is that everyone in society is entitled to have a fair and equal chance at basic rights and resources, such as housing, medical treatment, use of public transportation, use of public spaces like malls and restaurants, and perhaps most importantly, the opportunity to be employed and paid a fair wage.

Summary

The broader social issues that affect us as members of society include poverty, alcoholism and drug abuse, domestic violence, and racism and discrimination. These problems have high social and economic costs, including increased health care costs, crime and unemployment. They are also complex problems that are not easy to solve, despite social programs, addiction treatment centers, welfare systems and government spending.

Social problems are often linked and may create "vicious circles" for those who are affected by them. For example, sociologists have found that victims of domestic violence are more prone to commit violent crime, abuse drugs or alcohol, be chronically unemployed, or become abusive towards family members themselves. Likewise, people with drug or alcohol abuse problems are more likely to have fatal traffic accidents, commit theft or assault, or have trouble holding down a job.

What's clear is that these problems are prevalent in our society and affect us all. Understanding them can help us appreciate the effects they have on our own lives and those of the people with whom we come into contact.

Key Terms

Term	Definition
Absolute poverty	The condition of earning less money than what the government defines as the minimum to have an adequate standard of living. According to the U.S. government, a person living alone is in absolute poverty if their annual income is less than three times the minimal cost of food for one year.
Alcoholism	A disease caused by regular abuse of alcohol despite negative consequences. Alcoholism often has physical, psychological, and social symptoms.
Corporal punishment	A form of punishment in which bodily pain is inflicted on a person. A common form of corporal punishment is spanking.
Discrimination	Discrimination can be defined as unfair treatment of individuals because of an assumption about who they are and how they will behave. In discrimination, a person is prejudged on the basis of their background and not their personal abilities.
Domestic violence	Abuse that takes place between family members, partners, or ex-partners. The abuse could be verbal, physical, sexual, or damaging in some other way.
Drug abuse	Use of drugs in a way that is harmful to one's health or against the law.
Physical abuse	A form of domestic violence characterized by assault, physical violence, or threats or gestures that cause a person to feel unsafe.
Poverty	Generally, the condition of having very little money. See **absolute poverty** and **relative poverty**.
Prejudice	Prejudice is a preconceived opinion that is based on stereotypes or rumors about a different type of people, not on actual experience.

Key Terms

Term	Definition
Racism	Racism is the belief that a person's race is at least partially responsible for his or her individual abilities or limitations. Racism could also be the belief that one race is superior to others.
Relative poverty	A state of poverty in which a person earns less than half of what the average person earns in a year. Relative poverty varies depending on where a person lives.
Sexual abuse	A form of domestic violence in which there is unwanted sexual contact. It also includes sexually related threats or humiliation, or other actions intended to coerce a person into sexual activity.
Verbal abuse	A form of domestic violence that includes spoken attempts to humiliate a person or erode their dignity or self-esteem.

CHAPTER 5

Social Issues in the Workplace

Highlights of the Chapter

This Chapter Covers:

- Discrimination in the workplace, including nondiscriminatory hiring policies, wrongful dismissal, and affirmative action programs

- Sexual harassment in the workplace and guidelines for its prevention

- Absenteeism and its financial and personal consequences

Introduction

Chapter 4 described the major social issues that affect society in general. This chapter describes the major social issues that concern the workplace directly and the laws and guidelines designed to prevent these problems or at least reduce their occurrence. These issues are employment discrimination, sexual harassment in the workplace, and absenteeism.

Just as discrimination, unfair biases, and prejudices affect society at large, they also affect the workplace. Employment discrimination refers to discriminatory employment practices, such as bias in hiring, promotion, job assignment, termination, and compensation. In many countries, including Canada and the United States, laws prohibit employers from discriminating on the basis of race, color, sex, religion, national origin, physical or mental disability, or age. There is also a growing body of law preventing employment discrimination based on sexual orientation or gender identity.

Sexual harassment is any behavior of a sexual nature that causes another person to feel uncomfortable. It may include unwanted touching, threats, teasing, or any sexually related, inappropriate activity. Laws exist to protect employees from sexual harassment and to give those who are the victims of it alternatives to quitting their jobs. Sexual harassment is seen as a violation of a person's basic human rights.

Absenteeism means failing to show up for work when there is not a legitimate reason for being absent, such as calling in sick when you are in good health. Absenteeism is a growing problem that is estimated to cost businesses billions of dollars a year in lost productivity.

Discrimination in the Workplace

Employment discrimination can have detrimental effects on people's jobs, careers, and financial status. For example, it may:

- prevent a qualified person from being hired

- restrict a person's opportunity for advancement

- lead to an unjust dismissal

- lead to a person being laid off, when, based on seniority or other factors, someone else should have been selected first

- lead to attempts to dismiss someone or find an excuse for terminating their employment, before they are able to reach retirement age

Employment discrimination can also lead to unfair compensation. In some parts of North America, employers are notorious for hiring illegal immigrants because such people can be paid less than the law provides and they are not in a position to come forward and make complaints for fear that they will be sent out of the country.

There are now strict laws in place in the United States and Canada to prohibit all of these practices, and these laws are increasingly being enforced vigorously and effectively. There are tribunals that hear

complaints, based on violations of human rights, when people are refused employment or housing, unjustly dismissed from employment, or when they have suffered from some other tangible effect of discrimination.

Nondiscriminatory Hiring Policies

Most major employers in North America now have hiring policies that are designed to prevent personnel officers from making decisions based on racist or prejudicial attitudes. There are now a wide range of questions that are not permissible for an employer to ask during a job interview or on a job application.

For example, listed below are some examples of questions that employers in most parts of North America may <u>not</u> ask on a job application or in an interview:

- Are you married or single?

- Where were you born?

- What is your religion?

- Do you belong to any political groups, parties, or societies?

- How old are you?

- Do you have any children?

- What does your spouse do for a living?

- How much money does your spouse earn?

In some jurisdictions, it is not even permissible to ask if you have ever been arrested, if you have ever been refused credit, or to probe into your past or personal background at all, other than to ask details of employment and education. As a general guideline, the only information you are required or expected to provide is the names and addresses of previous employers, and places where you have attended school or taken courses.

It is often difficult to prove that you have been the victim of discrimination during hiring, though such suits are increasingly being brought forward successfully. If you did not get a job and someone else

did, this does not necessarily mean that the other person was selected because of discrimination. However, if the other person who was selected is clearly less qualified than you for the position, then a strong case can be made that discrimination was a factor.

Wrongful Dismissal

When people are unjustly dismissed from their employment for reasons of racism or discrimination, it is sometimes easier to make a case. Today, employers are expected to keep written records of dismissals in the workplace. The only form of dismissal that need not be carefully documented is a layoff, which is strictly defined as a shortage of work. There are also rules in place for how layoffs must be conducted, particularly in unionized workplaces. The selection of those employees to be dismissed should not be arbitrary.

Aside from layoffs, virtually all other types of dismissals are based on some form of conflict between worker and employer. These are commonly known as firings. Today, when a person is fired, companies are expected to keep proper records that demonstrate unsatisfactory performance. In some cases, employers are required to give employees written warnings about unsatisfactory performance prior to giving notice of dismissal.

Increasingly, employees are successfully winning wrongful-dismissal lawsuits against employers. However, employers have ways of protecting themselves from this type of legal action. One option is to have a written employment contract that makes it clear that the employer has the right to dismiss employees on certain grounds. But employment contracts do not take the place of labor laws, nor do they give the employer the right to dictate any and all terms to the employee. The courts will look at an employment contract, but they will overturn any provisions of it that are illegal, discriminatory, or unreasonable.

In the past twenty years in both the United States and Canada, there have been a wide range of laws enacted to prohibit discrimination and to ensure both fairness and safety in the workplace. These laws have attempted to ensure that people have a fair opportunity to obtain work and that they are not dismissed from their jobs arbitrarily or

unfairly. The laws also attempt to take on underlying historical biases and prejudices within society and to lessen their impact on the workplace.

Affirmative Action

Sometimes labor laws have gone farther than merely prohibiting unfair practices. For example, a strategy known as affirmative action requires many government employers and large industries that deal with the government to hire more women and people of different races or ethnic backgrounds. An affirmative action policy encourages employers to select minorities and women ahead of other similarly qualified individuals. The goal of affirmative action policies is to allow groups that have historically been victims of discrimination to gain better opportunities.

Affirmative action programs have at times led to ill feelings because they appear to favor individuals who are less qualified for a given position simply because they are members of a minority group. This may be seen as a form of reverse discrimination.

Proponents of affirmative action concede that, on occasion, this will happen and in individual situations it may sometimes appear to be unfair. However, they assert that the greater goal of achieving fairness across the entire organization or industry is more important than some of the decisions that must be made in specific cases.

Affirmative action programs have a broader ideal or goal in mind than merely settling a specific employment issue. Many people believe that racism and discrimination will not be eliminated in our society until people become accustomed to seeing people of other races and cultures or the opposite sex in virtually every role within the workplace. When we have more black, Hispanic, or female police officers, bankers, executives, nurses, teachers, lawyers, and so on, gradually everyone in society will be brought up in an environment where they do not automatically associate certain positions or privileges with people of certain races or characteristics. Once this is the case, it will be easier for long-held biases and prejudices to be set aside and for people to be treated as individuals, with equal opportunity and fairness.

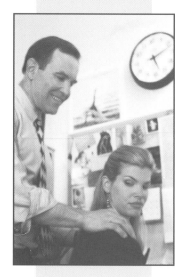

Sexual Harassment

Sexual harassment has become an important issue in the workplace. Sometimes people accused of sexual harassment defend themselves, believing that the rules have gone too far or are excessively strict. They do not believe that they have assaulted anyone or violated any legal or moral code, and they don't understand why they are being reprimanded.

The fact is that sexual harassment laws and guidelines are not merely designed to protect employees from being physically attacked or fondled. It has always been against the law to force oneself upon another person sexually, or to use threats to force a person to perform some sexual activity against their will.

These things are forbidden in the workplace and have always been so. However, sexual harassment as it is defined today goes much farther than this. The intent is to prevent a person's sexuality from interfering with their ability to do their job, or to feel comfortable and secure in their work setting. The intent is not just to prevent assaults, but to prevent sex from becoming an issue and a problem.

Most employees, when they come to work, prefer to be able to concentrate on the job for which they have been hired. They would like to be able to leave their sexuality behind and not have it crop up as an issue or a distraction. While they are doing their jobs, employees do not want to be constantly compared to one another on a sexual basis. They do not want to be the butt of sexual jokes, and they do not want to be ostracized or treated unfairly because they do not wish to flirt or engage in discussions of a suggestive nature.

Guidelines for Prevention

For this reason, modern guidelines for preventing sexual harassment are considerably tougher than they were just a decade or two ago. They now include such categories as off-color jokes and cartoons, unwanted teasing, and unwanted mention about the size or shape of a person's body—in short, anything that causes sexual tension or distraction.

Sexual harassment runs a gamut in severity from incidents that are mildly annoying or distracting to those that are so upsetting and

stressful that they can force a person to quit a job. Sometimes there is a progression from milder to more severe incidents. This is why, particularly in large companies, supervisors are now receiving extensive training on the topic of sexual harassment and how it must be managed and controlled. Like absenteeism, sexual harassment is a serious problem that cannot be dismissed lightly. The problem cannot be dealt with unless the standard is applied uniformly at all times and to all individuals.

At its most flagrant and serious form, acts of sexual harassment are designed to force or pester employees into participating in sexual acts. A boss may overtly request that a coworker have a sexual relationship with him, or may simply perform a series of gestures that are intended to be strongly suggestive of sexual interest. If the harasser is rebuffed at first, the tactics may change somewhat. The harasser may be tempted to use his position of authority within the company to retaliate against someone who has rejected his sexual overtures, threatening them with dismissal or lack of promotion, or simply saddling them with an unfair number of undesirable assignments as a punishment. Frequently, such retaliatory action causes so much distress that an employee feels forced to leave a job they would otherwise have been happy to continue.

Laws are now in place to give harassed employees alternatives to having to quit. It is now possible to confront a supervisor or coworker who is harassing you and to get outside assistance, since sexual harassment is seen as a violation of a person's basic human rights. A person who has been dismissed as a result of retaliation for refusing sexual advances can now sue an employer and win compensation.

The problem arises when the acts of harassment are more subtle or less forceful in nature. Sometimes people who commit acts of harassment do not understand that this is what they are doing. They think that they are merely being friendly, or that they are pursuing someone with whom they would like to have a personal relationship. A person accused of harassment in the workplace may be flabbergasted and ask a question like "Well, is it a crime now to ask someone out on a date?"

In society, it is generally acceptable to ask someone if they would like to go out on a date. In the workplace, however, there are some

restrictions on doing this. Some companies have had so much trouble with this issue that they have forbidden employees from dating one another. Dating among employees is sometimes referred to as fraternization, and some companies expressly forbid it. They may even require employees to sign a contract that states that they will not engage in it.

Even if there is no such policy in your workplace, you must use considerable care and discretion in attempting to begin a romantic relationship with a coworker. For one thing, you must be willing to take no for an answer. It may not be harassment to ask someone on a date once, but to do so over and over again once they have refused may be viewed as harassment. You may be making this person uncomfortable, which could affect their feeling of security and well-being in the workplace.

After all, a person who is on the job is somewhat of a captive audience. Someone who is not your coworker who did not wish your advances could simply avoid you or refuse to take your phone calls. However, if you and another person work for the same company, there may be very little that person can do to physically remove themselves from your unwanted advances. This is why a stricter guideline must be applied to protect workers, since they are in a situation where they are vulnerable, and where they have a lot to lose if a situation becomes intolerable for them.

Another issue related to sexual harassment is touching. Handshaking has always been an acceptable form of touch in many business situations. However, all other forms of touching should be discouraged in a work setting. At times, putting one's hand on another person's shoulder may seem an innocent gesture, but it is one that is increasingly open to misinterpretation. You should consider that it is no longer acceptable in today's workplace for you to put your hands on another employee for any reason. This applies not only to males, but also to females. Although most sexual harassment cases involve male employees harassing female employees, this is not always the case. Some women have developed flirtatious gestures such as putting their hands on a man's arm when they are talking to him or offering playful hugs or other gestures that involve physical contact.

Finally, there is the issue of language with regard to sexual harassment. There are many slang and vulgar expressions that involve sexual acts or sexual areas of the body. This language is considered inappropriate in the workplace and indeed in most social settings today. When a male employee uses this sort of language around female coworkers, it may be interpreted as a sign of disrespect or even hostility. Because such terms are often thought to demean women, using them in the presence of female workers is a way of reminding them of sexual differences and making them feel insecure or vulnerable.

Sometimes sexual harassment is deliberate and insidious. There have been notorious cases of harassment reported in situations where the first female employees were finally allowed into such settings as industrial plants, police forces, the military, or other traditionally male domains. Women have been systemically harassed and tormented in the effort to drive them out of private academies or other institutions that some men believe ought to be reserved for males only.

These are the blatant, well-publicized cases where the issues are fairly clear-cut. The problem is that for every one of these serious and unquestionable cases there may be a thousand other situations where the harassment is more subtle. Most women report that they experience some form of sexual harassment during their working lives. Thus, this is not an issue that involves only a few, and only those in unusual work situations. It has become an everyday problem to which all employees, whether male or female, should give some thought and discussion.

Absenteeism

Absenteeism is a problem that is often underappreciated by young people who first enter the workplace. One reason for this is that in the past decade many public school systems have either willingly or inadvertently softened their standards on school attendance. Principals and teachers are now more tolerant of students who miss school without a good excuse. In some cases, it is merely a lack of ability to enforce the rules, as the problem has grown to proportions that often defy the ability of school administrators to keep track of individual students day by day.

One problem with a lax standard of attendance in public schools is that it sometimes leaves young people caught by surprise when they enter the working world, where the standards are not only tougher, but are both enforceable and enforced. In a public school, students are part of a large crowd that must be dealt with sometimes as though it were a single entity. School students can get lost within a crowd, or within a peer group, and the individual attention paid both to their achievements and transgressions is reduced.

The Financial Consequences of Absenteeism

When young people enter the workplace, however, they enter a one-on-one world. They are hired not as a group, but as an individual. Employees work for one specific company, and usually for one specific supervisor. The work for which they are hired is of considerable importance to their employer; if it weren't, the employer would not be spending the money on the employee's wages. When employees fail to do their work, there are financial consequences for the employer. Companies will not be able to survive unless they pass those consequences along to employees, when it is appropriate to do so.

The problem of absenteeism in the workplace can be somewhat compared to a school of piranha attacking a large animal in a lake or river. Individually, each fish takes rather small bites. However, the cumulative effect of all of the bites taken by all of the fish can be devastating. Absenteeism costs businesses billions of dollars a year. It is often their single most significant and definable cause of loss.

In large corporations, the losses are so severe that people are hired specifically to deal with absenteeism. Considerable time and money is invested training supervisors to enforce company policies and deal with violations. However, in small businesses, absenteeism can be even more harmful. It may not merely be a case of having to spend extra money to have the work done by other people. There could be a loss of income that may prove irreplaceable and that, if prolonged, could even threaten the livelihood of the business.

Consider the following example. If a store has three employees to serve its customers, and one of them misses a shift on a busy Saturday without finding a replacement, the store is left to function with only two workers. This obviously makes for an unpleasant day for the two

people who will have to work extra hard that day, but it has additional consequences that the person who failed to show up may not have considered.

The employee who stays home may assume that the store will actually come out ahead because they may not have to pay him or her for the shift. However, the store actually stands to lose far more money than it would have saved. It's possible that the store would be so busy that the lineups would discourage people from coming in and shopping there on that particular day. Hundreds or even thousands of dollars worth of business may be lost as people walk into the store, see the lines, and walk out to shop elsewhere. Furthermore, some of the customers who do stay and wait may become annoyed and frustrated, and this may affect their shopping decisions in the future. The next time they need something the store sells, they might remember the lineup and decide to go elsewhere.

Of course, every time that one employee stays home from work, there may not be this sort of direct and measurable loss to the business. However, business owners know that, over time, small losses add up. This is why almost every business owner has decided they must adopt a tough policy on absenteeism. There is always the fear that if an owner becomes lax with enforcement, the problem will increase, and that a person who is successful in skipping work one day will look for other opportunities to do so in the future. There is also a legitimate fear that if an employee is allowed to get away with this, then other employees will be resentful, or may be motivated to skip work themselves.

Breach of Trust and Contract

There are other, more subtle reasons why absenteeism angers and annoys business owners, sometimes to a greater extent than young employees are able to understand. When an employee fails to show up, or calls in sick when there is reason to suspect that he or she is not, a breach of trust and a breach of contract occurs. When you accept employment with an organization, you are entering into a contract with the person or organization hiring you, even if you don't sign a written contract. You are guaranteeing your services in return for your salary and other benefits.

In return, the employer is demonstrating a certain degree of trust in you. The employer has chosen you over others in granting you the position. By allowing you onto its premises, it is trusting you with its money, its merchandise, and its good name. It is allowing you to be a representative for the company or organization in its dealings with customers. In a sense, the employer is undertaking the same type of risks as though it were allowing you into a family of sorts.

When an employee is absent without excuse from work, employers often feel violated. They feel that the sense of trust has been betrayed. They may feel that they have been conned or duped by statements and behaviors that the employee showed during the job interview, but that are no longer evident. Right or wrong, they get the sense that the employee is trying to pull a fast one on them. In a sense, the employee is stealing something from them by dishonoring the agreement that has been made. There may be economic consequences for the business by the employee's failure to show up, but even if there are no obvious consequences, the feeling of betrayal can still be there.

The other problem with absenteeism is that it suggests the employee is not committed to working for the company. It suggests that the employee would rather be elsewhere, that the work is of little interest, and that the employee feels no sense of duty to perform it. The larger problem with this is that it leads the manager to wonder if the employee will be performing well even when he or she does show up the next time. A person who has tipped their hand that they don't want to be there is someone who needs to be watched closely, even when they do finally come back to work.

You may be thinking to yourself that this is an awful lot to read into one sick call. It should be pointed out that absenteeism refers to unjustifiable absences from work. People get sick, and a serious sickness is a proper excuse for being absent, provided that it is reported and documented according to company policy. The situation becomes classified as absenteeism if the employee is not sick, or is only mildly ill, and could be or should be at work, particularly when there is an element of deception involved in making an excuse for the absence. Defined this way, even a single event of absenteeism is cause for concern. Once any sort of pattern develops, most employers will view the situation quite seriously.

The other problem with absenteeism is that it is subtly addictive. The employee who stays home from working at the store one Saturday may be sorely tempted to do it again the next Saturday or at some other point in the near future. Some employees want to stay home to do other things, such as engage in recreational activities with their friends. Others stay home out of laziness, because they want to sleep in or because they have been out late the night before. Sometimes employees stay home simply out of depression or frustration with their job and dissatisfaction with their work situation.

When absenteeism is the result of dissatisfaction or frustration with a job, it is a symptom of another problem that must be dealt with. If you are unhappy at work, you must address the causes of this unhappiness and sometimes bring them to the attention of your employer. Staying home is not a good way to deliver a message. Also, it may well turn your employer against you and make them ill disposed to consider your perspective on any issues or grievances that you may have. If something is bothering you that makes you not want to go to work, it is important that you try to talk to someone and identify the problem and what can be done about it.

Absenteeism may seem like an immediate release, but it can have lasting consequences. It may go on your record, which may follow you from one employer to another. If a reference check reveals that a prospective employee was frequently absent from work in the past, this information can have almost as devastating an effect as proof that a person stole from his employer. The prospective new employer will fear that they would be taking on a known problem case, and it is something they would rather avoid doing, particularly if there are other candidates for the job who do not have this blot on their record.

✴Summary

Employment discrimination, sexual harassment in the workplace, and absenteeism are major social issues that affect today's workplace. In many countries, including the United States and Canada, laws exist to protect employees from discriminatory human resources practices and sexual harassment. In addition, most major employers in North America now have hiring policies that are designed to prevent personnel officers from making decisions based on racist or prejudicial attitudes. Some employers are even required to specifically target groups that have historically been victims of discrimination for job and career opportunities. Affirmative action programs strongly encourage many government employers and large industries that deal with the government to hire more women and people of different races or ethnic backgrounds.

Sexual harassment is seen as a violation of a person's basic human rights. Many employers have strict policies to help prevent its occurrence and send the message to employees that it is not tolerated in the workplace.

Often caused by job dissatisfaction or frustration with a job, absenteeism is a growing problem that has high costs for large companies and small businesses alike. These costs arise from lost productivity and reduced capacity to provide products and services to customers, resulting in dissatisfied or even lost customers. Excessive absenteeism also has personal costs for the employee. It can become a blot on your employment record, and result in lost job opportunities when employers decide not to hire you due to concerns about your reliability.

Key Terms

Term	Definition
Absenteeism	Failing to show up for work or school when there is not a legitimate reason for being absent.
Affirmative action	A policy that encourages employers and colleges to select minorities and women ahead of other similarly qualified individuals.
Discrimination	Discrimination can be defined as unfair treatment of individuals because of an assumption about who they are and how they will behave. In discrimination, a person is prejudged on the basis of their background and not their personal abilities.
Employment discrimination	Employment discrimination refers to discriminatory employment practices, such as bias in hiring, promotion, job assignment, termination, and compensation.
Sexual harassment	Any behavior of a sexual nature that causes another person to feel uncomfortable is sexual harassment. It may include unwanted touching, threats, teasing, or any sexually related, inappropriate activity.
Wrongful dismissal	The term "wrongful dismissal" describes a situation in which an employee's employment contract is terminated by the employer in circumstances where the termination breaches terms of the contract or employment law. Examples of wrongful dismissal include dismissal based on: ■ a wrongful cause, ■ discrimination, due to such factors as race, gender, sex, or age, or ■ retaliation for filing a workers' compensation claim or for reporting illegal employer activity.

CHAPTER 6

Attitudes That Promote Human Relations Success

Highlights of the Chapter

This Chapter Covers:

- Productivity

- Honesty and ethics

- Courtesy

- Positive thinking

- Team participation

- Leadership

Introduction

In this chapter, we focus on specific issues and attitudes that affect our success in human relations, both at work and in our personal lives. These attitudes for human relations success are:

Productivity, which means being a productive worker, with a strong work ethic and the desire to produce high-quality work;

Honesty and ethics, which means being honest and ethical in your dealings with clients, coworkers, and supervisors and following the general ethical standards that apply to all work situations;

Courtesy, which involves being courteous to clients, coworkers, and supervisors, and adopting the standards for courteous communication followed at your workplace;

Positive thinking, which means striving to maintain a positive outlook on life to maintain or improve your mental health and quality of life;

Team participation, which involves building effective relationships in the workplace by being a team player and communicating effectively; and

Leadership, which involves developing leadership skills and qualities, if progressing to a management or supervisory role is important to you in your career.

Adopting these attitudes and behaviors will enable you to build effective relationships with others and create a positive impression with employers, both of which are important for success in any career.

Productivity

Productivity is a significant buzzword in the working world these days. As it is used by business management specialists, it means work efficiency. It is not a measure of how long someone works, or even how hard they work, but rather of the end results: the useful benefits that come out of that work. In order to be measurable, productivity is usually related to a unit of time. For example, a secretary who types five letters in one hour is considered more productive than a secretary who types five letters in two hours, provided that the quality of work is comparable.

Quality is an important factor in productivity. Simply being faster does not make you more productive. You may be faster than someone else, but if you are making mistakes and some of your work has to be corrected or discarded, then your productivity suffers.

In the workplace, cost is also a factor in assessing productivity. Even if you make something faster and better than someone else, if you spend a lot more money doing so—more than can be recovered successfully through the sale of the goods—then the operation is not considered productive.

The concept of productivity has many relevant applications throughout the working world and also in our personal lives. Productivity can be applied to personal goals and our relative success in achieving them. A person who has no goals has no way of measuring productivity. Whatever they accomplish each day, there is nothing against which to measure it. If they have no plan for the day,

they cannot judge whether its activities were particularly successful, particularly unsuccessful, or just mediocre.

It is important to consider what personal attributes and social skills contribute to making a person productive at work or at home. The first of these is a sense that time—one's own time as well as the time of other people—is valuable and ought not to be wasted. People who say things like, "You only live once," or "Life is too short," are reflecting an attitude that there is much worthwhile that can be achieved in the world, but a limited time in which to do it.

Such people tend to get out of bed in the morning and quickly get going. Even if the day's plans only call for doing the laundry or other domestic chores, they prefer to get their chores done as quickly as possible, so that they will have more time later to do other things that may be more important or enjoyable.

Having a Strong Work Ethic

The other essential attribute that fuels productivity is something commonly known as a "work ethic." People with a strong ethic feel a sense of responsibility for keeping themselves busy and trying to do worthwhile things with their life. If people with a strong work ethic find themselves sitting around doing nothing, they tend not only to feel bored and frustrated, but also a little bit guilty. Their sense of themselves and of their own worth is largely tied up in the tasks that they are able to accomplish.

Whether a day's work involves building a house, writing a novel, teaching first graders, or keeping a clean and attractive home and looking after children, the person with a strong work ethic likes to feel tired at the end of the day. They are content to know that the reason that they are tired is because they made an effort to do something that needed doing.

Employers look for people who are productive and who have a good work ethic. There are certain basic traits or components of one's personality that indicate a person is likely to be a productive worker. For one thing, as previously mentioned, a productive person hates idle time. For a productive worker slack time is always the most difficult to get through, because it tends to pass the most slowly. A productive person likes to keep busy, not only because of their work ethic, but

because it makes the day more pleasant and seems to help it go by more quickly. When you keep busy, you don't notice the clock as often. Before you know it, it is break time or lunch time, or quitting time at the end of the day.

People who have learned this basic lesson about working life tend to be more contented, so they stay at their jobs longer. While they are working, they also tend to be more cooperative, be more agreeable, and get more accomplished.

Producing Quality Work

Another trait that employers look for in employees is a desire to please, to impress, and to demonstrate one's capabilities. These traits lead a worker to try to produce quality work, which will be noticed and praised by others, and to find more efficient ways of doing things. Such a worker takes pride in the work the company turns out and the image and the reputation that their work conveys to customers.

Consider this example: You are working at a restaurant as a waiter or waitress. You believe that the restaurant provides good-quality food at reasonable prices and that it is better than its competitors. Therefore, you take pride in your work. It is important to you to do your tasks correctly in order to maintain the company's image and reputation. With these attitudes, you are a productive employee. You are careful in handling food. You make sure that portions are standard and that presentations are attractive. You pitch in and help out where needed, when backups or minor crises arise.

Conversely, perhaps you don't really want to be working at the restaurant, or don't really believe that the company provides anything of value of which you can be proud. In this case, you will tend to see your shifts as an endless fight against the clock and against your supervisors. Your objective may be to do as little as possible, short of being reprimanded or dismissed. When no one is looking, it may not particularly matter to you whether the item you are preparing is properly cooked or sufficiently fresh or attractive. Your mind will tend to be elsewhere.

Such a situation cannot endure over the long-term. Either you will become so bored and frustrated that you will quit on your own, or your

supervisors will eventually detect that you are not a conscientious worker and they will take steps to replace you.

The important thing about productivity is that it is really a win-win situation. If you are more productive at work, your employer comes out ahead, but so do you. You tend to be happier. You tend to feel better about yourself. You experience less boredom and less stress. You receive more praise and less criticism and, all in all, your working life is a much more positive experience.

Honesty and Ethics

The term ethics refers to conforming to proper standards of behavior accepted by the majority of people who work in a particular profession or trade. Almost every job and profession has a code of ethical conduct. Lawyers are expected to follow a set of rules when advertising their services or billing their clients. Doctors and clergy are expected to follow codes of confidentiality and respect for personal dignity and privacy. Stockbrokers and financiers are expected to follow codes of conduct with regard to disclosure of accurate information and safeguarding the best interests of their clients. Housepainters are expected to do honest work following quality standards. Auto mechanics are expected to charge reasonable prices for the work they do, and not to falsify records concerning their labor or what components need to be replaced. These are but a few of the many examples of professional ethics in our society.

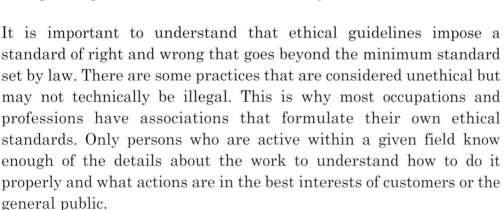

It is important to understand that ethical guidelines impose a standard of right and wrong that goes beyond the minimum standard set by law. There are some practices that are considered unethical but may not technically be illegal. This is why most occupations and professions have associations that formulate their own ethical standards. Only persons who are active within a given field know enough of the details about the work to understand how to do it properly and what actions are in the best interests of customers or the general public.

Ethical standards are enforced not merely out of a sense of doing the right thing. Professional associations, whether of lawyers, accountants, pet store owners, or funeral directors, work to ensure that their profession maintains a positive image within the eyes of the

public. They understand that when someone has a bad experience with one member of their profession, the word gets out and bad publicity can hurt all members of the profession, even those who always follow ethical standards.

People who do the same type of work as you care about how you do it because they see your work as reflecting on them. If you do a poor job, it is not just your problem. It may make customers or the public lose faith in the industry or business. Once the company's reputation has been tarnished, the self-esteem of everyone who participates in similar work may be affected.

A dishonest auto mechanic makes all auto mechanics appear less admirable in the eyes of the public. Cumulatively these dishonest practices create suspicion, ill feelings, even jokes or sarcastic attitudes that may be magnified and passed along by people like comedians or journalists. If enough auto mechanics behave dishonestly, before long being an auto mechanic will not be a very attractive career choice. Because honest mechanics don't want to see this happen, they have an interest in denouncing the dishonest minority within their trade.

General Ethical Standards

There are some basic business principles that apply to all workers, not only to those within a specific profession or industry.

> **The following is a general listing of typical ethical standards that would apply to almost any line of work:**
>
> - It is unethical to claim to have done work that you have not done or to claim to have done it in a different manner from the way in which it was actually executed.
>
> - It is unethical to lie to a customer about the nature of a problem, to invent a problem that does not really exist, or to deceive a customer about the severity of the problem and the urgency of addressing it.
>
> - It is unethical to take credit for work that you did not personally do, or to vouch for work you are not sure was actually accomplished.

- It is unethical to take on work for which you are not adequately qualified, particularly if there are formal qualifications prescribed by law or community standards. For example, it is unethical to do electrical wiring for someone if you are not a licensed electrician. In a retail store, it is unethical to issue a refund or make an exchange for a customer if you are not the store manager or someone who has been given the authority to make such a decision. It is unethical to speak for the owner of the store or to invent a store policy simply to help you deal with customers.

- It is unethical to take anything that does not belong to you home from work, unless you have been given specific permission to do so. This applies not only to merchandise, but also to things such as office supplies, reusable containers, packaging materials, fixtures, or anything else that belongs to your employer.

During the time for which you are being paid to work, you have an ethical obligation to perform work that is of direct benefit to your employer. It is considered unethical to take long breaks from work, other than the designated lunch and coffee breaks.

For example, if you accept a lengthy personal call while at work, you are depriving your employer of your services. Your employer is paying you for that time, but you are not using that time to your employer's benefit. This is a form of stealing. If the company pays you $10 an hour, and you spend half an hour on the phone making a personal call, you are essentially stealing five dollars from your employer, because you are being paid for time when you are not actually working.

It is unethical to be absent from work without a valid excuse or to falsify an excuse. As mentioned earlier in the text, even if you aren't paid for the time when you are absent, you can still hurt your employer by leaving them short of the staff they need to adequately run their business on that day.

It is unethical to make dishonest statements to customers, supervisors, or fellow workers. There are any number of examples that would apply here. Telling a customer that a product can do something that it cannot do is one example. Telling your supervisor that you did something that

you did not actually do is another. Telling a customer a false statement about a competitor would be an additional example. You may be able to get away with these things once or twice, but if you develop an attitude of dishonesty, it is almost inevitable that you will get caught and that the incident will come back to haunt you.

Consequences of Unethical or Dishonest Behavior

It is important to understand that relationships in the working world are often more fragile than those in one's personal life. If you lie to your sister and you get caught at it, there may be some bad feelings for a while, but eventually things will probably be smoothed over, and the relationship will return to normal. There are certain personal relationships in our lives where we tend to be accepted for better or for worse, and our faults may be accepted or overlooked if we don't push them too far. You cannot count on this being true in the working world. Sometimes one serious mistake is all that you are allowed to make before an employer loses confidence in you and looks to replace you.

The other problem with unethical or dishonest behavior in the workplace is that there are often legal ramifications to be considered. If you lie to a customer about a product that ends up being defective and causing some harm to the customer, you leave yourself and your employer liable to a lawsuit. In addition, companies often prosecute people for shoplifting or for pilferage (internal theft of items by employees).

In short, the working world is not a place where you can expect people to forgive and forget. If you do not approach your job with the correct attitude, you place yourself at risk of losing it. It is really that simple.

Courtesy

Rules of courtesy can be seen as a third logical extension beyond the law and beyond ethical standards. They are a further dimension to society's expectations for our public behavior. It is possible to get away with minor breaches of courtesy once in a while. If you are discourteous once, you are more apt to be forgiven if you give an assurance that it will not happen again. However, like infringements of ethics, infringements of courtesy add up to create an image of you that may eventually sabotage your career.

Standards of courtesy may vary significantly from one work setting to another. However, it is important to understand that the rules of courtesy in any given situation are something that you must study and adopt. The standards of courtesy with which you are quite comfortable at home or with your friends may not be satisfactory in many job situations. A higher standard may very well be expected. This is especially true in businesses that deal with the public, such as stores, restaurants, hotels and the like.

At home, if your brother suddenly calls out to you asking you to do something, you might feel quite comfortable shouting back to him, "Not now, I'm busy!" This might be an acceptable reply between you and your brother. However, the very same comment could get you into considerable trouble in some work situations. A customer might consider such a comment so rude that he or she will report you to your manager, who will call you in to explain your conduct.

Higher standards of courtesy apply in many situations within the working world. For example, it is almost never acceptable for a waiter or waitress in a restaurant to tell a customer that they are too busy to do something. In many cases, it is also considered discourteous to call out to the customer from across the room, rather than to go over personally and find out what they want.

Being Courteous to Customers and Coworkers

One difficult aspect of the rules of courtesy for new employees to understand is that often there is a double standard in place. Customers may get away with being discourteous to you, but this does not give you the right to be discourteous back to them. The old saying, "The customer is always right," is not always true, but it is worth thinking about. There is a distinction between the person or company that is paying money for a service and the person or company who is receiving money in order to provide the service. Customers usually receive certain privileges in return for their money. This does not give them the privilege of being rude, insulting, or humiliating, but it does mean that their standard of courteous behavior may be a little different from yours.

If a customer in a large department store calls out to you from a couple of aisles away, this may be annoying, but it may not be considered to

be a serious lapse of courtesy. However, if you do the same thing, shouting back at the customer, your supervisor may well criticize you for it. This is one example of the double standard. It may not seem fair, but it is a fact of life in the working world.

Given the complexity sometimes involved in courtesy guidelines and the levels of courtesy that are expected in different workplaces, how can you know what is or is not acceptable behavior? The number-one rule of thumb is to take careful notice of how other employees perform in the same situation. Adapt your standards to what you see around you. Get in the habit of talking to customers or coworkers in the same way that you see other employees doing, particularly those who seem to be the most admired or successful.

Here are additional examples of discourteous behavior that apply to a wide range of work settings:

- It is discourteous to interrupt someone while they are speaking, unless there is some urgency in getting their attention.

- It is discourteous to raise your voice when speaking with a customer or a supervisor. It is also discourteous to use harsh language or to take a tone that might be considered insulting.

- It is discourteous to continue to do other things while you are talking to a customer or answering a question. Unless there is some immediate reason why you cannot do so, stop what you are doing, look the customer in the eye, and give them the benefit of your full attention while you are speaking with them.

- It is considered discourteous to speak to customers or supervisors while you have food in your mouth, while you are chewing gum, while smoking a cigarette, etc.

- It is considered discourteous to leave a person waiting on the phone for more than a minute without getting back to them. It is also discourteous to leave a person waiting more than a couple of minutes if you walk away from them to get product or information in a store. If it takes longer than that to find what you are looking for, or to obtain the answers that the

customer is seeking, apologize for the delay and indicate that you need a little more time.

- In many situations, it is considered discourteous to argue with your customers. If there is some reason why you cannot do what they want you to do, explain the reason. But do not get involved in an argument, and certainly avoid criticizing them for their attitude or behavior. Be sure that discussions, particularly those that are difficult, do not degenerate into personal attacks or insults. Sometimes you have to say no to a customer. Sometimes the customer will become angry, hostile, or even verbally abusive as a result. This does not give you the right to behave in the same way. Your own behavior is often expected to hold to a higher standard.

A good example of the higher standard of behavior expected of employees involves health care workers in hospitals. Patients or relatives sometimes take out their frustrations on hospital staff, making comments that are unfair and uncalled for. However, health care workers are expected to make some allowance for the stress and discomfort that these people may be feeling at the time. They must keep their cool and respond courteously.

Positive Thinking

The importance of positive thinking is gaining renewed emphasis these days in the fields of psychology, business management, meditation, spirituality—and even medicine. It has been discovered that patients with serious illnesses improve their quality of life if they maintain a positive outlook and the determination to fight and win against their disease.

Many people misunderstand what positive thinking is all about. They may see it as a naïve and overly optimistic viewpoint, where everything in the world is rosy and people should be happy all of the time. This is not the attitude to which we are referring here. Most reasonable people acknowledge that life can be difficult at times. They understand that we will all undergo periods of suffering and that we must be continually vigilant to protect ourselves from harm.

People who practice positive thinking may vary greatly in their personal philosophies about the meaning of life or how much happiness one can expect to find. However, what they share is a determination that however good or evil the world around them may be at any moment, they are going to do their best to make the most of it. They are determined to use the opportunities that come their way, to minimize the dangers and the losses, and to make the best life for themselves that they can.

Another element in the philosophy of positive thinking is not to become your own worst enemy. In other words, don't let your own attitude and negative thinking add to the troubles that you may already have. It is bad enough when the rest of the world seems to give you a hard time. However, when you end up giving yourself a hard time by dwelling on negative feelings or depressing attitudes, then you take whatever is wrong in your life at the moment and actually make it worse.

The fact is, despite suffering in the world, people in general and in North America in particular can expect to lead long, healthy, and productive lives. Today, we can expect to live on average into our seventies, and we can expect a reasonably high standard of comfort and security for the better part of those years. We can expect to survive long enough to get married, have children, and to see our grandchildren. Most of us will be able to find employment, earn enough to afford our own homes or comfortable apartments, and purchase our own vehicles. We will have enough free time to entertain and amuse ourselves with a wide range of activities and interests. We will have the opportunity to develop friendships, to fall in love, and to enjoy many of the good things in life.

At no other time in human history have we enjoyed better overall health, a better chance at being able to recover from accidents or illnesses, and the ability to keep pain and suffering to a minimum in most cases. Yes, there are problems, there are challenges, and there will be many difficult moments. The purpose of positive thinking is to make sure that we are ready for them and that we can do our very best to prevent them from interfering with the "good life," which we have every reason to expect will be available to us most of the time.

The other thing that practitioners of positive thinking understand is that our life is not only what we make of it, but also what we choose to see in

it. People in our society are in the common habit of courteously asking, "How are you?" whenever they run into someone they know. Some person may be in the habit of answering, "Fine," regardless of how he or she may actually be feeling. Others may take the question literally and see it as an opportunity to make it clear that they are not feeling well, that they are not happy, and that something is wrong with their lives.

These two individuals may have virtually identical situations in life: a lot of good things going for them, but one or two significant problems with their personal life, finances, or health. However, the person who feels a need to complain constantly is no doubt suffering much more from the very same problem or malady than the person who attempts to shrug it off and get on with their day. What's more, the person with the more positive outlook tends to be better liked and respected by others.

Guidelines for Practicing Positive Thinking

The following paragraphs present some basic guidelines for practicing positive thinking in your daily life, both at work and in your personal life.

Focus on What's Going Well

Concentrate primarily on what is going well in your life, rather than what is wrong. You cannot shove your problems under the rug, but do not spend a disproportionate amount of time thinking and worrying about them. Analyze them, deal with them as best you can, then try to put them out of your mind.

Most of us may be in a situation where 80 to 90 percent of our life is essentially going well, and only 10 to 20 percent of it is difficult or unpleasant in some way. However, we may spend 80 percent of our time thinking or worrying about the 20 percent that isn't as we would like it to be. When we do this, we fail to appreciate what is going well for us. We are effectively crowding the good things out of our life by not allowing ourselves to enjoy them.

Deal with Your Fears Effectively

Many people can become overwhelmed or incapacitated with dread or fear. The fear may be directed at a specific person or event, or it may be more general. General fears involve things such as a fear of developing a serious illness, being involved in an auto accident, being a victim of violent crime, and so on.

There are several effective strategies for dealing with fears and not allowing yourself to be swallowed up by them. The first is to assess how realistic the fear is; in other words, how likely is the danger actually to arise? Your odds of being involved in a plane crash are very slim. Your odds of being violently attacked may be either very slim or very high, depending on the neighborhood where you live. The odds may be increased if you travel alone at night or leave yourself vulnerable in some other way.

Separate the "irrational" fears from the ones you need to pay attention to. In a sense, no fear is totally irrational in that the things we are afraid of do really happen somewhere in the world to some people, or we would not have developed a fear of them. However, some scenarios are so unlikely that we would do well to put them out of our minds. If they should happen, then we shall deal with them when the time comes. But they are not worth preparing ourselves for ahead of time. There are more important things to be concerned with.

Once you have determined that your fear is reasonable, determine whether or not there is anything you can do about it. Can you improve the locks on your home or apartment, install more smoke detectors, or change the route you take to come home from work at night if it takes you through a risky area? Is there something you can do about your health problems? Can you have yourself tested or screened to allay a particular fear you might have about your health?

If there is some preventive action you can take, then doing so will make you feel better about yourself and help reduced your fear. On the other hand, if there is nothing you can do, you must accept this fact and try to prevent yourself from dwelling needlessly on the source of the fear. What you must avoid are dead-end thinking patterns, where your mind goes endlessly over the same events or anxieties, without coming to any useful conclusions.

Another way of dealing with realistic fears is to imagine the worst-case scenario. In other words, if absolutely everything you feared were to happen, what would you do about it? How would you cope, and how would you survive? For example, if you are afraid that a nearby river will one day flood and drive you out of your home, then imagine the event actually occurring. Imagine moving in with a relative for a

while. Imagine returning to your home later and getting your friends and neighbors to help you clean up. Imagine applying for insurance benefits or possible government-assistance programs to help you get started again. Imagine having gotten through all that and being back in your home safe and secure once again.

If you can picture yourself surviving such a catastrophe—and the catastrophe hasn't even happened yet, and may never happen—then you know that you are prepared for the worst. You know that no matter what, you will not be defeated. There will always be somewhere to turn, some way to cope. If you can come to this understanding, your fears will be much more easily managed—particularly the lesser fears that are nowhere near as catastrophic or important.

Set Achievable Goals

Often negativity shows itself in imprecise feelings of depression, frustration, or a general sense that things are not the way you would like them to be, but you don't know how or why. One way to overcome this tendency is to start being more specific about what you want or expect, not just over the long-term, but on a daily basis. Set yourself an achievable goal each day, something that will take you one small step closer to what you want. At the end of the day, if you have met your goal, you can feel some satisfaction in having done so. If not, you can always try again the next day. You can feel successful in life only if you are able to identify specific and reasonable areas in which you hope to succeed.

Maintain a "Big Picture" View

Positive thinkers try not to lose sight of the "big picture" when little things do not go their way. As an example of how to apply this thinking to everyday life, imagine having a minor traffic accident with relatively little damage and no injuries. Such an experience is inevitably frustrating, no matter how it occurred. It means your day is going to be disrupted. You are going to have to stop and attend to this matter. You are not going to get where you were going. The rest of your schedule will have to be rearranged. If the other person was at fault, it may be difficult not to be angry with them, even though you may have made a similar mistake yourself at some time in the past.

At times like this, the challenge is to step back a little bit and look at the big picture. You are still alive and well. Neither you, nor any

member of your family or friends were hurt. You have insurance and your car will get fixed. You still have a car, you still have a life. All of the good things that were in your life when you woke up in the morning are still there. Compared to the sudden death of a loved one, a catastrophic accident, a disabling injury, or another serious trauma, what you have just experienced is not such a big deal after all.

You have two choices on how to get through it. You can keep as positive an outlook as you can, do what needs to be done as quickly and efficiently as possible, and then try to put it out of your mind. Or, you can let yourself get very angry and depressed, and let the incident ruin your entire day. Either way, the car is damaged and will have to be fixed. The price that you end up paying is significantly greater, however, when you allow the incident to drag down everything else in your life.

Hold Yourself Accountable for Efforts, Not Results

Finally, a very important rule of positive thinking is to accept the fact that you will not always come out a winner. Do your best, then accept whatever happens. Hold yourself accountable for efforts, but not for results. Often results are partially or even entirely beyond your control. You are not going to win them all. Not every day is going to go smoothly. The positive thinker has bad days just like everyone else does. However, over an extended period of time, the positive thinker has fewer bad days, and those that he or she does experience are not nearly as depressing and debilitating.

Team Participation

Up to now, much of this chapter has discussed personal attributes, goals, emotions, and behaviors. In the workplace, it is also important to view our own role and actions in a larger context. When we join others in working toward a common goal, our role must mesh with the other players on our team in order for our contribution to be meaningful and truly effective.

One weakness that many people have, even those who are bright and fundamentally hard working, is that they look at every situation in terms of only personal benefits. They are excessively eager to advance their own cause and reputation, or to take credit for success. They are reluctant to share their knowledge with others or to help out others, unless they see some direct benefit to themselves.

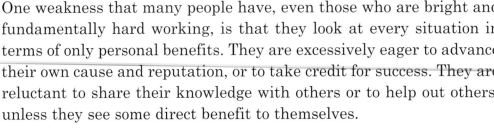

The problem with these attitudes is that cumulatively they actually conspire against the individual's personal success. Over time, such persons manage to alienate others around them. They may even find themselves in a situation where others are working against them or doing things to deliberately make life difficult for them.

It is human nature for us to want to be given credit for our accomplishments and to be appreciated for the work that we have done. Skillful managers know how to give such personal recognition, while still managing to keep their employees focused on the organization's goals and the well-being of the team as a whole. By showing your supervisor that you are a team player, you are willing to help others and to do whatever is necessary to accomplish the group's objectives, you will usually find that you will be rewarded with an excellent rapport with your supervisor.

Sometimes supervisors actually value the willingness to be a team player above and beyond individual skill or personal achievements. You need not be phenomenal or exceptional if you are able to fit in well, meet the basic expectations of other members of the group and help get the job done.

How to Be a Team Player

In order to be an effective team player, there are several basic habits and attitudes to adopt. For one thing, you need to be attentive and a good listener. Pay attention to what your supervisor and the other members of your team tell you. Try to focus not only on the team's tasks, but also on the purposes behind the tasks and the overall goals of the organization. If you understand what the organization requires in order to succeed, then your own work assignments will have more meaning to you. You will have a better appreciation of how the work needs to be done to satisfy the requirements of coworkers or customers.

Another important thing is to communicate well at all stages of the working process. This means giving or receiving instructions and information before, during, and after the job itself. Don't make assumptions. Make sure that others are aware of any information that may be important to them.

The final thing that is needed to be a good team player is some degree of patience and self-control. Occasionally someone else on the team

may say or do something (either deliberately or accidentally) that rubs you the wrong way, hurts your feelings, or wounds your pride. It is important not to react to such events immediately in the heat of the moment. By doing so, you risk sidetracking the group into a personal confrontation that detracts from the focus on group goals.

If you have a problem with a member of your team, and do not feel you can resolve it directly by discussing the situation with that person, talk to your supervisor. However, do so with discretion. Pick the right time and moment. Avoid public criticism of the other employee. Make it clear to your supervisor that your objective in speaking to him or her is to settle the matter, so that the work of the team can proceed more smoothly. Your goal is not to complain or to get revenge on the person who is causing you difficulty.

Remember, too, when criticizing anyone, to focus on behaviors, not on personality. Do not criticize the individual; criticize the actions that you feel are less than desirable, and offer suggestions for alternatives. This is what is meant by constructive criticism, which focuses on finding solutions rather than raising complaints.

Leadership

Employees who do a reasonably good job of practicing all of the human relations skills discussed in this text will soon find themselves in a situation where new options and opportunities become available to them. One of these opportunities may very well be the chance to take on a leadership role within the organization where you work. If advancement to a supervisory or management position is one of your long-term career goals, it is important to take a moment to consider what traits and qualities are considered valuable in a leader. These are the basis on which your performance will be judged as a leadership candidate.

Not all good workers make good leaders. Some people mistakenly believe that if they are successful at their jobs, they will eventually advance into some supervisory or managerial capacity. This is not necessarily true. You need not feel that you have failed or that something is missing in your life if this is not the direction in which your career takes you.

Progressing to a Managerial or Supervisory Role

If you are interested in being a leader, it is important to consider the qualities that are necessary for success and your motives for wishing to lead. Many people associate leadership roles with earning extra income. Managers tend to make more money than the workers whom they supervise. Sometimes people strive for promotions purely for the extra income involved.

However, progressing to the level of supervisor or manager will bring significant changes into your working life, and income is only a small part of that change. It is important to understand what some of the other changes will involve, because you cannot achieve long-term success as a leader unless you are happy in that role. Along with the rewards come new areas of responsibility and potential for stress. It is important to understand what you are getting yourself into if you choose to go this route.

When you become a leader within an organization, you take on increased responsibility for helping the organization to achieve its goals. You are expected to put the company's requirements first, which is not always an easy thing to do. Sometimes it means stepping away from the camaraderie of the other workers.

Qualities and Attitudes of a Leader

As a leader, you will have to make tough decisions. You will have to criticize other people's work, and sometimes even take disciplinary action against them. You are not always going to be liked and appreciated for taking these steps. Thus, it is important that you maintain some degree of personal detachment from the workers you are assigned to supervise. Some supervisors are not able to do this. They feel the need to be friends with everyone, and this is often one of the most serious drawbacks or deficiencies in a new leader. We all want to be liked, but sometimes you need to have enough confidence in yourself that you can do what needs to be done, whether or not it makes you popular.

Another quality that is necessary in a leader is the ability to be objective about your own performance and those of other people around you. Self-evaluation is critically important. You must not automatically become defensive whenever you are challenged or criticized. You must

be able to weigh both sides of an issue. If someone else is right and you are wrong, you need to be able to admit to this fact. What ultimately matters is finding solutions to problems, not worrying excessively about whether you come across as the culprit or the savior.

Leaders do not need to be liked by their employees, but they need to be respected. You must be competent at your job. You must be well prepared and hard-working if you want other people to do the same. You must lead primarily by example. You must be firm at times, but you also need to be fair. You should explain your actions and decisions, so they do not seem to be arbitrary or dictatorial.

Communication skills are some of the most essential qualities for good leadership. You need to tell people clearly what you expect of them and not make assumptions. You will also need to give them feedback on how they are doing, including both constructive feedback when they are making mistakes and praise when they are doing well.

One of the most difficult aspects of being a leader is that the success of your projects is at least partly beyond your control. In order to succeed, you need to get other people to perform for you. You cannot do it on your own anymore. If you cannot influence other people to do their jobs well, then you will fail as a leader.

This can be a sobering and humbling thought. As a leader, you are no longer self-sufficient in your job. You need other people to work for you and with you, or you have no hope of succeeding. All of the human relations skills that we have discussed in this text become absolutely critical once you step into a leadership role. If you cannot get others to respond the way you want them to, you cannot be a leader; it is as simple as that.

If leaders have any particular expertise, above and beyond the technical field in which they work, it is that they are human relations experts. They have mastered the lessons that have been briefly presented here and put them to use to their advantage. They are successful because they understand success and what is necessary to achieve it. They are able to teach and inspire others and help them develop their own technical and human relations skills.

Summary

The issues that affect success in human relations on an individual level include productivity, honesty and ethics, courtesy, and positive thinking. Productivity, which means work efficiency, is a measure of the end results or products that come out of work. Although productivity is usually related to a unit of time, quality and the costs associated with work are also important. People who enjoy and take pride in their work tend to be productive workers who contribute to their employer's success. People who are highly productive are said to have a strong work ethic.

Almost every job and profession has a code of ethical conduct. For example, lawyers, doctors, clergy, accountants, and stockbrokers all have codes of ethical conduct they are expected to follow in their daily work. There are also general ethical principles that apply to most work situations.

Rules of courtesy can be seen as a third logical extension beyond the law and ethical standards. They are a further dimension to society's expectations for our public behavior. Standards of courtesy vary significantly from one work setting to another. The standards of courtesy in the workplace tend to be higher than the ones we follow with family and friends, particularly in service industries such as stores, restaurants, and hotels.

The importance of positive thinking is gaining renewed emphasis in the fields of psychology, business management, meditation, spirituality—and even medicine. Positive thinkers focus on what is going well in their lives, rather than what could be better. They also don't allow life's misfortunes or the occasional negative experience to affect their outlook on life.

Summary

The issues that affect human relations success on a group or team level include team participation and leadership. Team players pay attention to what their supervisor and team members tell them, focus on the team's tasks, and contribute to achieving the overall goals of the organization. Effective leaders are respected by the employees who report to them, and are able to communicate expectations clearly and get employees' cooperation. They are also objective about their own and others' performance, open to constructive feedback, and willing to accept that others may sometimes be right.

Key Terms

Term	Definition
Courtesy	Behavior that is polite, respectful, and considerate. It is practiced with good manners and kindness toward others.
Ethics	Moral principles that guide behavior. In general, ethics are standards of right and wrong that are agreed upon by society.
Leadership	Leadership involves the ability to affect people's behavior to accomplish a goal or mission. A leader must earn respect in order to influence others.
Professional ethics	The principles of conduct governing the behavior of a professional group.
Positive thinking	A strategy for success that involves focusing on what is positive in a situation, instead of dwelling on what is negative.
Teamwork	Working with others to achieve a common objective.
Work ethic	A belief in the moral benefit of hard work.

CHAPTER 7

Stress and Frustration

Highlights of the Chapter

This Chapter Covers:

- What is stress?

- Stress in the workplace: its causes and symptoms

- How to deal with stress effectively, so it doesn't affect your health

Introduction

Stress has become a popular topic in recent years. Not only professional counselors, but also people in general are becoming more aware of it and its impact. It is not clear if our lives are any more stressful than those of our parents or grandparents. However, we are beginning to appreciate better how stress can rob us not only of our health, but of success in our human relations endeavors.

This chapter defines what stress is, including its causes, symptoms, and impact on mental and physical health. It also discusses the nature of stress in the workplace and how to deal with stress effectively, through self-care, goal setting, and self-evaluation.

What Is Stress?

Stress is the condition that results when we perceive that there is a discrepancy between the demands of a situation and our ability or resources to deal with it. Stress takes many forms; different people express and react to it in different ways. There are a variety of causes and a variety of symptoms. With some stressful challenges, like moving into a new home or studying for a final exam, we may feel stressed for a while, but then we feel relieved and satisfied once we have achieved our goals. This kind of stress is rather healthy, because

it builds character and leads us toward self-actualization. Stress becomes negative when accumulated psychological distress manifests itself both in physical responses and in emotional and behavioral changes.

Stress is often created by a large number of minor problems and events whose individual effects begin to accumulate. There may be one overriding factor, such as a personal relationship that is not going well, or it may simply be the ongoing wear and tear of day-to-day events.

When we interpret a stimulus as stressful, we generally respond in three stages. First we feel alarmed and possibly afraid. Our muscles tense up and our blood pressure rises, while we react to the stressful situation. This is known as the alarm stage.

Next, we resist the cause of the stress. We try to put up with the problem, but doing so leaves us weaker and less prepared for any other problems. This stage is called resistance.

Finally, responding to continued stress leaves us exhausted. Exhaustion is the stage that usually comes to mind when we think about what it means to feel stressed. We might feel tired, anxious, depressed, bored, afraid, frustrated, or hostile. The exhaustion stage of stress is also sometimes referred to as burnout. A person who experiences burnout often has psychological symptoms like feeling depressed, emotionally detached, or generally disinterested. They usually also have physical symptoms, like a weak immune system, a sleep disorder, or chronic high blood pressure.

Often, we feel stressed from our personal lives and our careers at the same time, or the stress from one part of our lives makes us less prepared to handle other problems. Stress can leave us weak and prone to sickness, which can add to our difficulties.

Stress in the Workplace

Due to a sense of lack of control, job pressures create stress for many people. Workplace stress is the physical and emotional response that occurs when there is a poor match between job demands and the capabilities, resources, or needs of the worker. Some jobs are more

stressful than others by their nature. If a person's work involves more than the typical amount of pressure, danger, responsibility, or the need for attentiveness, then stress will be a factor, even in a job that is going reasonably well.

Workplace stress can cause depression, anxiety, job dissatisfaction, fatigue, tension, and maladaptive behaviors, such as aggression or substance abuse. These conditions may lead to poor work performance or even injury. It has been well documented how stress contributes to health problems, such as headaches, stomach disorders, and even chronic illnesses such as high blood pressure or cardiovascular disease.

Some people also experience more stress than others in the same circumstances. The amount of stress that we experience is related to our sense of ourselves, our confidence in our ability to deal with situations, and to the mechanisms that we have developed to relieve ourselves of the stress that builds up within us.

Stress and Interpersonal Relationships

It is important to realize that stress can have an equally devastating effect on the success of our human relations efforts. When stress builds up to intolerable levels, it often tends to erupt in ways that can damage our relationships with others. These eruptions or reactions to stress may be out of proportion to the situation, seem inappropriate, and be misunderstood. It is not just that there is a chance that we will say or do something that will offend or anger someone else. Some ramifications are more subtle. For example, any public display of our succumbing to stress, or our less-than-ideal ability to cope with it, may be viewed as a blemish on our character.

People don't want to associate with, let alone have as employees, people who are extremely emotionally erratic—calm one minute, flying off the handle the next. Unpredictability and uncertainty are not things that are valued or even well tolerated in our society. Most employers would rather put up with someone who is somewhat of an underachiever if they are consistent and predictable, than deal with someone who is full of surprises in terms of their moods and emotions, regardless of how well they may perform in their better moments.

This points out the importance of doing what we can to handle stress in our lives. It is seldom practical to eliminate from our lives all of the things that tend to cause stress. Life is almost by its very nature stressful. If you don't feel at least some stress driving a car across the city during rush hour, you are probably not sufficiently aware of the real dangers that demand your attention. Driving is sometimes pleasant, but it is often stressful for all of us. Furthermore, we all get sick, and this is not pleasant for any of us. Sometimes we have more serious health problems that may require hospitalization, surgery, or some extended and possibly unpleasant treatment. We experience the sickness and eventually the death of the other members of our family and other people we care about. Our jobs don't always go smoothly. Our personal relationships are not always easy. In other words, at least once in a while, something is going to happen that is partly beyond our control going to cause us to experience more stress than we are comfortable with handling.

Ignoring the situation does not often work. Pretending that we are not stressed out does not usually work either. The only way to handle stress is to accept the fact that it is real and develop a strategy for relieving it, before it becomes overwhelming.

Addressing Boredom

One factor that is often underestimated in causing stress and frustration is the deceptively simple topic of boredom. As compared with fear, acute anxiety, or pain, boredom can seem like a relatively mild form of discomfort. However, if it is persistent, it can have an unexpected degree of influence over our moods and actions.

Boredom can be viewed as a form of self-evaluation about our lives. It is the internal sense that what we are doing is not satisfying. Something is missing. We are understimulated, undermotivated, and distinctly underenthusiastic about ourselves and how we are living our lives.

We all get bored on occasion. We all have to do work that we find tedious. That is not what we are discussing here. The problem arises if when we get home and we finally get the free time that we were looking forward to, we still find ourselves bored. If this consistently happens to you, it is a sign that you need to take some time out and rethink and possibly restructure some areas of your life.

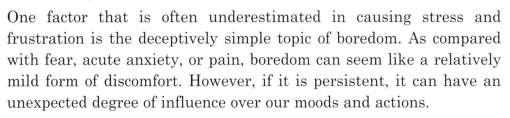

People tend to be bored when they do not have sufficient understanding of themselves. They have not set goals for themselves. They do not know what they want, and consequently they have difficulty figuring out how well they are doing and how happy they are or ought to feel about their lives. The simple act of setting and pursuing goals—not just career goals, but goals about relationships, or even goals about recreational activities— is one good way to alleviate boredom. It also helps to develop a sense that one's life is valuable and one's time is limited, and to become determined to make the best possible use of the free time that is available.

One problem with boredom is that it is frequently misunderstood. When a person doesn't take some responsibility for their own boredom, they may tend to blame it on others. I am bored because my job is pointless. I am bored because my spouse or girlfriend isn't satisfying me. I am bored because I don't have the opportunities or attributes I see in someone else.

As long as you continue to blame another person for your boredom it will express itself in frustration and resentment. You will fail to take the internal steps that are necessary to get to the root of the problem and do something about it. The best way to view boredom is to see it as your own problem. It is not something the world is doing to you; it is something that you are doing to yourself.

If you are laid up with a cast in a hospital bed, boredom may be inevitable, because you have limited resources to change your situation and engage in other activities. Under most other circumstances, however, you do have the ability to change your situation. It is your responsibility, not the responsibility of other people, to do so. Only you can determine what you want and need to be contented in life. Although you may need other people to help you achieve these things, other people can't figure them out for you. What pleases them may not please you. They cannot respond to your needs if you do not fully understand them yourself.

Sometimes it is worth getting outside help from counselors if you have particular difficulty coming to grips with a general sense of boredom and dissatisfaction in your life. Professional counselors have seen hundreds of people in similar situations, and they may have learned ways of identifying the problem and coming up with creative and practical solutions.

Dealing with Stress

There are various things we can do to reduce the stress that we feel in our lives. Some of them involve trying to improve the situations that cause the stress, if there are realistic ways of doing this. However, others involve simply taking time out from the situations that are giving us trouble. We all need to have outlets, little escapes once we are home and on our own and have free time at our disposal. We need to have hobbies and interests, things that intrigue and excite us, things that we look forward to doing. Preferably, some of these should be physical activities, outdoor experiences, or athletic events.

Athletic activities provide several benefits, both physically and psychologically. They tone our muscles, increase our circulation, and improve our respiratory and circulatory systems. This allows us to sleep better and to have every system in our body function with greater efficiency. That in itself is a help in coping.

There are often subtle and simple ways of relieving stress in our day-to-day lives. Simple things such as taking a hot bath, lighting a pleasantly scented candle, listening to music you enjoy, or brightening up your room with eye-pleasing colors can each have surprisingly positive effects. Like stress itself, the positive things we do to cope with it are also cumulative. A lot of very little things can add up to making a big difference.

Particularly during times that are very stressful, we need to treat ourselves. There is the old analogy about the horse that is made to pull the cart because its owner hangs a carrot on a stick in front of its nose. The point of the carrot idea is that we need to have something out in front of us, something that we can see, something that we can obtain in the near future that motivates us to keep going during tough times.

After a tough day, decide to go out for dinner to treat yourself, either by yourself, with a friend, or with your family. Plan interesting and pleasant events on the weekend, so that you can unwind from a long work week. If you are feeling particularly low, treat yourself to a long-distance phone call with someone whose voice and conversation are always reassuring. Within reason, set aside a portion of your budget for picking yourself up at lower moments and enjoying some recreation or entertainment. If waiting for the weekend isn't good

enough, consider going out to a movie on a weeknight. If you are too tired to cook, order a pizza.

In other words, be good to yourself. Cut yourself some slack. Give yourself a break, a chance to rest and recover. If you do so, you will find that you do not exaggerate your problems and become overwhelmed by them. You will have more self-control in your dealings with others, and you will be able to project a positive disposition when doing so. In this way, you will not fall victim to what we discussed in the previous article—taking a difficult situation and making it worse. Whatever difficulties life throws at you, you will avoid adding yourself to the list and becoming your own worst enemy.

Goal Setting

In earlier chapters, we have briefly mentioned the topic of goal setting. Goal setting is important not only in the workplace and our professional lives, but also in our personal lives as well. Unless we set goals for ourselves, not only are we less likely to live up to our potential, but we will also have trouble figuring out how well we are doing. We need standards against which to measure ourselves, and goals provide them for us. Goal setting can help provide us with a sense of achievement and reduce our stress by making our lives more productive and manageable.

In order for goals to be helpful, they must be positive and realistic. We need to set goals over various time frames. We may have long-term goals, such as to own our own home within the next five years. There may be medium-range goals concerning where we would like to be in the coming year.

However, it is also important that we set short-term and even daily goals. When we wake up in the morning, it is helpful to have some sense of what we would like to have accomplished by the end of that day. Such daily goals, again provided they are realistic, help to give us a sense of satisfaction with our day. When we have accomplished our goal, we have a good feeling. The day seems a success, and at the end of it, we are able to unwind and relax without feeling frustrated or dissatisfied.

Goal setting is also a way of taking larger tasks and dividing them up into manageable bites. If you have a large task that must be completed

during the coming week, such as packing all your belongings in preparation for moving, such a task may seem overwhelming. You may have a tendency to put it off until you have no alternative but to scramble to get it finished. By dividing the task up into daily goals, each of which will handle a portion of the total workload, the task becomes more manageable. You can avoid feeling stressed out, frustrated, or overwhelmed by having to look at the total project all at once.

Self-evaluation

This text has no doubt given you a lot to think about with regard to potential for self-improvement and becoming more effective in your human relations efforts. However, there is one fundamental issue or attribute without which it would be impossible for you to benefit from anything we have discussed here. You need to be open to the prospect of change, and you need to be willing to evaluate yourself critically to explore areas of weakness and areas for improvement. The self-evaluation process works, together with goal setting, by identifying areas of possible self-improvement for which personal goals can be set.

Some people are so insecure and defensive that they are almost never willing to admit that they are wrong about anything or have any weaknesses. The fact of the matter is that we are all wrong some of the time, and we can all improve as human beings. In fact, people who are fundamentally secure, happy, and successful tend to be the most self-critical because they do not see the criticism as a threat. They are not afraid to look in the mirror. As a result, they are more likely to notice things about themselves that can be improved.

Objective self-evaluation is never an easy process. Many people find the key to doing it well is being attuned to how other people—friends, relatives, and coworkers—see you and react to what you do. An opinion someone else has about you is not necessarily a correct one, but it is certainly something that is worth taking a close look at. If you find that more than one person reacts to you in the same way or seems to share the same opinion of you or your work, then there is a good chance that there is something to what they are saying. They may not understand you completely. There may be factors that they are unaware of. However, if they have a problem with you, then you have a problem that needs to be addressed. Denying that the problem exists is not going to enable you to solve it.

It is particularly useful to listen and consider the opinions of individuals who are somewhat detached or objective—persons with whom you do not have a close relationship that may cloud their view of you. This is one of the important reasons that many people turn to professional counselors at critical moments in their lives, when they feel the need to make a change or when they are experiencing a particularly stressful or difficult situation.

However, the heading of this topic is self-evaluation, not evaluation by others. You must take the feedback you receive from others, sift through it, and consider it carefully. What ultimately matters is your own assessment. You cannot be handed your assessment by someone else. They can contribute only bits and pieces. You are the one who needs to put the puzzle together.

For self-evaluation to be effective, it needs to be a priority, and you need to set aside time to do it. It should not be something you do only when something goes wrong or when you experience a time of crisis. Whether you do it once a week, once a month, or once a year, it is valuable to sit down with a piece of paper and a pencil. Write down things about yourself that you like, then write down things that you don't like. Write down suggestions of ways that you might be able to change or improve those areas with which you are not fully satisfied.

At the same time, you can set some goals for yourself, including not only concrete goals, such as to save a certain amount of money in a specific time frame, but also personal goals concerning your relationships with others. At the end of any major project or cycle in your life, it is also a good time to take stock, evaluate how things went, and see what areas might be altered for the future.

The important thing about self-evaluation is that its only purpose is to help you look toward the future. You do not do it to reward or punish yourself for past achievements or mistakes. What has happened in the past is over and done with. What matters now is what you can take from those experiences to apply to your present and future activities and your interpersonal relationships.

Summary

Stress is the condition that results when we perceive that there is a discrepancy between the demands of a situation and our ability or resources to deal with it. Stress is positive when it leads to the accomplishment of personal or career goals and a sense of achievement. It becomes negative when accumulated psychological distress manifests itself both in physical responses and in emotional and behavioral changes.

It has been well documented that chronic stress contributes to health problems, such as headaches, stomach disorders, high blood pressure, or cardiovascular disease. For this reason, it is important that we manage and alleviate stress through regular physical exercise, taking time out from the situations that are giving us trouble, and doing things we enjoy outside of work.

Goal setting can help provide us with a sense of achievement and reduce our stress by making our lives more productive and manageable. Goal setting is important not only in the workplace and our professional lives, but also in our personal lives as well. In order for goals to be helpful, they must be positive, realistic, and tied to a specific time frame.

The self-evaluation process works, together with goal setting, by identifying areas of possible self-improvement for which personal goals can be set. Self-evaluation involves the careful consideration of feedback from others and, most importantly, your own assessment of yourself. The purpose of self-evaluation is to look forward to the future, rather than rewarding or punishing yourself for past achievements or mistakes.

Key Terms

Term	Definition
Alarm stage	The first stage in a reaction to a stressful situation, when we feel alarmed and possibly afraid, and our muscles tense up and blood pressure rises.
Burnout	A psychological term for the experience of long-term exhaustion and diminished interest, usually in a work context. Burnout often results from a period of expending too much effort at work while having too little rest and recovery.
Goal setting	Goal setting involves establishing specific, measurable, and time-targeted objectives.
Exhaustion	The final stage in our reaction to continuous stress, in which all the body's resources are depleted, and the body is unable to maintain normal function.
Resistance stage	The second stage in a reaction to a stressful situation, which involves resisting the cause of the stress. During the resistance stage, we try to put up with the problem, but doing so leaves us weaker and less prepared to deal with any other problems.
Self-evaluation	Self-evaluation is defined as the way a person views himself or herself. It is the continuous process of determining personal growth and progress.
Stress	Stress is the condition that results when an individual perceives that there is a discrepancy between the demands of a situation and their ability or resources to deal with it.
Stress management	Stress management involves using techniques to help us cope with or alter stressful situations, so they don't affect our mental or physical health.
Workplace stress	Workplace stress is the physical and emotional response that occurs when there is a poor match between job demands and the capabilities, resources, or needs of the worker.

CHAPTER 8

Common Errors in the Workplace

Highlights of the Chapter

This Chapter Covers:

Five common errors in workplace social interaction:

- Failure to listen accurately

- Underestimating others

- Failure to understand point of view

- Failure to understand what motivates others

- Permitting others to victimize you

Introduction

In order to improve how we relate to others in the workplace, or in any other area where we interact socially, it is important to study some of the common mistakes that people make. In most cases, these mistakes occur when people fail to communicate or to understand each other's motives. Yes, there are always a few no-win situations in life. However, a major objective of this text is to help you to better understand that usually when our interactions fall short of expectations, we have failed to take advantage of opportunities to communicate with coworkers and understand their point of view, or we have mismanaged those opportunities. In other words, the failures didn't have to happen. They were not primarily due to circumstances beyond our control. They were the results of decisions we made in the way we chose to interact with people.

This chapter describes five common mistakes in workplace social interaction and provides explanations for how and why they happen.

Failure to Listen Accurately

There are times when we all get caught not listening. Someone will be talking to us, and suddenly they will stop and look at us and say something like, "Hey, I'm talking to you. Are you paying attention?" These are the obvious failures to listen, the times when our mind is totally someplace else. What many people don't understand, however, is that even when our inattention is not so blatantly obvious that we get caught, we often fail to listen completely or effectively to what is being said.

The problem is that, most of the time, we don't get caught at it. Consequently, the conversation proceeds and comes to a conclusion without the other party realizing that only a portion of the message has been communicated. At least when someone stops and challenges us on our inattention, we get a second chance. In most real-life situations, there is often only one chance to get the message.

There are many reasons why we may fail to listen accurately to something that a supervisor, colleague, customer, or even a friend is trying to say to us. Sometimes it is simply a lack of concentration. If the message is somewhat difficult to grasp, or if it is being poorly worded or communicated in a roundabout way, we may tire of the mental energy that is necessary to hear everything that is being said to us. This tends to happen when we are being asked to do something we don't want to do, when the person trying to communicate to us is not someone we want to listen to at that moment in time, or simply when we are particularly tired or distracted.

There are several ways to avoid having this happen. They include making a conscious effort to face the person who is speaking to us, maintaining eye contact with them, and providing gestures, such as occasionally nodding, that indicate that we are paying attention. Another way to ensure that we are listening accurately is to reflect the message back to the speaker. Once the speaker has made an important point, we can restate the crux of that point in our own words to show that we have grasped it. You may say something like, "What you're telling me then, if I have it right, is that you are happy with the amount of work that I'm getting done, but you feel I'm still making too many little mistakes."

The other main reason that we often fail to listen accurately is that while the other person is speaking, we may become too involved in rehearsing what we intend to say in reply. This is particularly true when we feel defensive about what the other person is saying or when we disagree with it. In those situations, the focus of our attention is on arguing our own point of view. To some extent this is human nature, but we must guard against it, because while we are spending time formulating our argument, we may be missing key elements of what is being said to us.

If you are having a conversation with your supervisor, and the outcome of the conversation will be important in determining your status or situation in the workplace, it is far more important for you to be picking up as many clues as possible as to what is in the mind of your supervisor than to worry about instantly answering every challenge or argument. In fact, it may very well be to your advantage not to respond immediately to everything you hear with the first thing that comes into your mind. Doing so may only convince your supervisor that you are argumentative, set in your ways, and determined to defend your past behavior rather than listen to what needs to be done differently in the future.

One way to avoid rehearsing replies while other people are speaking is to get into the habit of pausing once the other person has finished, before asking a question or responding. Use the pause to consider your answer. This will free you from having to consider it while the other person is talking. It also conveys a positive image in that you make it obvious that you are thinking about what you have heard, opening your mind to it, rather than reacting immediately in a negative or a defensive manner. In some situations, you would actually be better off not responding immediately. Rather, you could say something like, "Well, you've given me a lot to think about. Do you mind if I mull it over a little bit? Maybe after lunch or tomorrow morning we can talk about it again and I can give you my reactions?"

Underestimating Others

Particularly when we enter a new social setting, we may be so focused on our own needs and problems that we fail to be perceptive in sizing up the other people with whom we are required to interact. The previous topic talked about a failure to listen. In some ways, underestimating others is a failure at observation.

When you walk into a new social situation, it may seem deceptively simple to you at first glance. Chances are it is actually incredibly complex. You are now becoming associated with a group of people who have been interacting for many months or years. The patterns to their interaction are well established and of considerable importance to them. As an outsider coming in for the first time, you may be perceived as a threat to the status or security of someone else who is already there.

People often react with a startling degree of aggressiveness when they feel threatened. However, that aggression may often take subtle forms. A person who feels threatened by you may try to undermine you behind your back, fail to cooperate with you, or even deliberately sabotage the outcome of some of your efforts, all the while maintaining a superficial cordiality when you happen to run into them in the hallway.

Another factor in underestimating others is making assumptions about what they do or the reasons they do things. Sometimes when you first enter a new work setting you may conclude that other people are not really working very hard, or that their jobs are not particularly important, or even that they don't seem to be particularly good at what they do. Sometimes you may be right, but more often there may be things that you don't yet know about what goes on in this organization and the reasons things are done the way they are. There is probably room for improvement in any organization. However, it is impossible to hope to achieve genuine improvement until you have a thorough understanding of how things have been done in the past and why they have been done that way.

When you are first hired for a new position, it is understandable and desirable to try to make your mark, and to show other people that you are a capable person and that you can contribute something positive to the organization. However, if you try to do this too quickly or aggressively, you will end up alienating other people who are already there. Moreover, the solutions that you propose may be simplistic or inappropriate because they are based on a limited understanding of the situation at hand.

Failure to Understand Point of View

The topic of motivation was discussed earlier in this text. It is important to realize that almost all human behavior has some

motivation behind it, and that motivations are very personal. For the most part, we are motivated to achieve personal satisfaction, success and security. In the workplace, as in any important social setting, we strive to advance our own cause, to be liked, accepted, appreciated, and rewarded.

You can expect that most of what people do in the workplace has this sort of personal advancement as its primary motivation. This applies not only to major projects or campaigns for promotion, but even to relatively minor aspects of social interactions. People are always trying to make allies, to increase their own importance within the organization, and to persuade others of the validity of their point of view. The main reason that human beings disagree so much in our society is that we often approach the same problem from different points of view and our self-interest takes us in different directions.

A Real-life Example: Labor versus Management

A typical example is a dispute between management and a labor union. A manager is hired, promoted, and achieves security by increasing the financial success of the operation. Thus, any situation that arises that might produce conflict between labor and management is viewed from that objective. The union representative, on the other hand, becomes popular and successful within his or her own peer group by improving the situation for the workers, increasing their earnings, increasing their long-term job security, and responding to other issues and concerns that they may have.

A manager and labor union representative may sit down at the table to talk about a specific issue, such as how to restructure a production area that is having difficulty. An argument may develop over technical issues, engineering problems, safety, job procedures, or something along these lines. However, the real issue is the manager's fear that the company will lose money if this problem isn't fixed, and the union representative's fear that the company may try to fix the problem by laying off workers or expecting them to take on more work in a given shift without being compensated for doing so.

These two people have different priorities and perspectives because their roles have given them each different experiences that have shaped their opinions. The manager has sat in on numerous

management meetings and has a good understanding of the company's goals and intentions. The union representative has not attended these meetings, and can only guess at what may have taken place there. Lack of knowledge can lead to uneasiness and suspicion. The union representative may read an ulterior motive into an innocent request.

Conversely, the union representative has had experiences in the workplace that the manager has not witnessed. He or she may have seen workers treated unfairly, or promises to them broken, perhaps over many years, experiences of which the manager may be ignorant. When they sit down at the table, these two individuals see things very differently because, in significant ways, they likely see the world itself very differently.

In issues of labor and management, the significance of point of view is rather obvious. However, it is important to realize that issues of point of view affect all of our relationships: discussions we may have with a spouse, a relative, a boss, coworker, customer, even sometimes with a casual passerby. We do not all see the world the same way, and we have different places and roles within that world. As a result, point of view is an important aspect to understanding why other people react to us the way they do.

Failure to Understand What Motivates Others

This common error in workplace social interaction goes hand in hand with the previous one, failure to understand point of view. However, in this case we are referring not to the general perspective that a person brings to a situation, but rather to the specific reasons why they behave the way they do in a given situation, or adopt the viewpoint or attitude that they do toward a specific problem. We often grow frustrated with other people because they seem at times to be unreasonable or illogical. People may appear to behave irrationally for no apparent reason, but they may be motivated by many predetermined factors. When we behave badly, we are often driven to that behavior by unpleasant past experiences and our fear of having them repeated.

The problem is that motivations are often subtle. Sometimes, we don't understand our own motivations, let alone those of other people. When

this happens, we may end up getting into an argument or disagreement, the subject of which is very different from the underlying cause. For example, a coworker may get into an argument with you about the way you are handling some specific task. The problem may not have anything to do with that task, but rather with the coworker's fear that you are trying to take over one of his or her privileges, trying to make him or her look bad, or doing something which will eventually cause more work.

A person is not likely to come right out and tell you any of these things. Therefore, they may attempt to get into a technical discussion about why what you are doing is incorrect, inappropriate, or undesirable. If the specific arguments they come up with are not particularly sound, you may decide to launch into an assault on those shaky arguments. In doing so, you may miss the point that it is not the arguments themselves that are the problem, but rather the insecurity or hurt feelings that are causing the other person to feel a need to invent these arguments.

It is important to analyze all of the critical conversations and the interactions in your life to at least make an attempt to determine their underlying motivations. Sometimes we do not know people well enough to understand what motivates them. Jumping to conclusions about their motivations can be as disastrous as ignoring their motivations in the first place. When we do not know what motivates other people, we should attempt to find out. We should attempt to steer conversations away from nonessential details and ask questions designed to uncover what it is that is really upsetting someone or causing them to feel a need to express a certain attitude or behavior.

Your Road Map

Think of it in the following way. Think of everything that you are and believe and want to do in your life as being copied down on a road map. Your road map will not only have specific routes and directions, but it will also identify landmarks. In other words, you have a certain view of your "neighborhood." By neighborhood, we mean the other people with whom you are associating. The routes that you take will make sense to you because of that neighborhood. There may be some parts of the neighborhood that are undesirable and which you seek to avoid traveling through. There will be reasons why you choose one route over another.

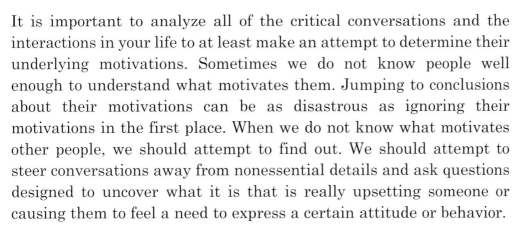

When we work with other people, we are in a situation where we have to play a role in selecting and navigating a route along which more than one person will be required to travel. The problem with doing so is that the people with whom you have to sit down and plan the route are not working from the same map. Each person has their own map that defines the realities and boundaries of their world. "Neighborhoods" that you see as undesirable may be attractive to them or may not even be on their map. Things that worry you or that you try to avoid may be things that other people actively seek and find desirable in their lives.

On the surface, we may all appear to be very similar. We eat the same food, we wear the same clothing, we drive the same cars, and we cooperate with one another in predictable patterns, timetables, and so on. However, under the surface, we are often much more different from one another than we may first appear. Our goals, values, and specific interpretations of the world around us can vary enormously.

Permitting Others to Victimize You

People associate the words victim or victimization with reference to criminal acts, such as being assaulted or having your home robbed or your property defaced. However, in a larger sense we fall victim to human relations acts in our everyday lives. Sometimes, these acts are deliberate attempts to harm us. At other times, they are the unintentional results of miscommunication or relationships that have gone awry.

What do we mean by being victimized? In the sense in which we are using the term, victimization refers to ongoing harm that is done to you and your ability to function successfully and happily in your environment. If you have a confrontation or argument with someone in the workplace, the incident may appear to be over when you turn your backs and walk away from one another. However, it is likely that the incident may have some ongoing consequences for one or both of you, and these consequences could cause you to suffer in some tangible way.

One of the obvious consequences of human relations failures is stress. You feel angry, hurt, anxious, or uncertain, and there are both physical and psychological consequences to these feelings. You may develop a headache or an upset stomach. You may become tired or

depressed, or have trouble concentrating. If your difficulty in concentrating causes you to have a serious car accident on your way home from work, then your victimization consequences will be every bit as drastic as if someone had pulled a gun on you in an alleyway.

Even if the consequences do not become that extreme, chances are that the ongoing anxiety, preoccupation, and stress will not only make you unhappy, but cause you to fail to function at your best. This might thereby provoke other incidents, perhaps involving other people who were not involved in the original confrontation. Thus, once again it is a case of a bad situation becoming worse. Because you are in a bad mood, because you are not concentrating, suddenly you have done something to get someone else upset with you, and your day is going from bad to worse.

An interesting point about victimization is that it really has nothing to do with who is right or wrong in any particular issue. You can be in the right, or even win an argument or a confrontation, yet still be victimized by the incident. The perfect example of this has to do with what is known as road rage. It has been discovered that motorists frequently become exceedingly angry at one another over what may be perceived as relatively minor breaches in courtesy on the highway. People have been known to make obscene gestures, to pursue other cars at high speeds, or deliberately cut them off—all in retaliation for a blunder which one believes that the other driver has made.

You become absolutely convinced that the other driver is an idiot and that your own performance is blameless, but who is the victim here? You are the one who is upset. You are the one who is losing control of your emotions. You are the one who is placing yourself in a situation where you are at risk of being seriously hurt or hurting somebody else. You have allowed yourself to be victimized by the other driver, who may never even know or understand what he did to cause you to become enraged.

The Dangers of Unresolved Disputes

Victimization is most likely to occur when there is no opportunity to resolve a situation or when one or both parties in a dispute walk away and deliberately leave the situation unresolved. An unresolved human

relations situation tends to seethe or fester. What may have started as a minor incident can turn into something that will cause an end to a relationship, once the two parties have cut themselves off from one another past what they consider to be the point of no return. Long-time friends have been known to break up over simple oversights, such as failing to be remembered on one's birthday. There may be a good reason for the oversight, but sometimes people keep their hurt and frustration bottled up and never let the other person know how they are feeling.

Pent-up feelings are very painful. When you allow other people to make you uncomfortable, and you do not act to resolve that discomfort, you participate in your own victimization. You cause yourself to become trapped in the anxiety, and to suffer its other tangible consequences, like the loss of a relationship, or even open hostility and retaliation by the other party.

The moral here is this: resolve your human relations crises. Regardless of who is right or wrong, chances are you will both suffer. Your own suffering will be a heavy price to pay for the element of revenge or vindication that you may feel you are deriving from shutting the other person out.

Summary

Do any of the five common errors of workplace social interaction apply to you and your workplace? Can you think of a time when your relationship with a coworker or supervisor could have gone better, if you had been aware of these common mistakes?

The next time you are interacting with coworkers or working on a team, consider what you can do to improve your communication and relationships in the workplace. Remember to listen accurately to what your coworkers are saying, without interrupting them or focusing on how you plan to respond. While speaking with coworkers, make eye contact and listen attentively. If you are not sure you have understood someone correctly, repeat back to the speaker what you have heard, in your own words, and ask for clarification.

To understand where others are coming from, it also helps to put yourself in their shoes. Try to understand your coworkers' points of view about a given situation and the motivations driving their behavior. Before making assumptions about what other people do or why they act that way, take the time to understand why current procedures and systems are in place at your workplace. Learn what you can about the organization's history and social culture. This will help you avoid oversimplifying issues and appearing too eager or aggressive to make changes and improvements before understanding the big picture.

Of course, you can't expect that your workplace relationships will always go smoothly; sometimes, you will experience conflicts with coworkers or a supervisor. To avoid unnecessary stress and anxiety, resolve these problems as soon as possible, rather than allowing them to fester and become worse.

Key Terms

Term	Definition
Miscommunication	The failure to communicate clearly.
Motivation	The reason (emotional need or desire) for engaging in a particular behavior.
Point of view	Also called perspective and viewpoint, our point of view is the personal context that shapes our opinions, beliefs, and perception of our experiences.
Road rage	An extreme case of aggressive driving, which tends to cause accidents on roadways. Examples of road rage include cutting others off in a lane, sounding the horn, tailgating, rude gestures, and verbal abuse.
Social interaction	A dynamic sequence of social actions in which people interpret what others are saying, respond accordingly, and attach meaning to a social situation.
Victim	In a social or political context, a victim is someone who is subjected to oppression, hardship, or mistreatment.
Victimization	The process in which someone is victimized in some way.
Victimize	To make a victim of someone. In social situations, people can allow themselves to be victimized by reacting in an emotionally charged way to what they perceive to be mistreatment by others and by failing to resolve ongoing conflicts.

CHAPTER 9

Mistakes and Adversity

Highlights of the Chapter

This Chapter Covers:

- The importance of admitting to mistakes in the workplace

- How to admit to mistakes in a professional manner that preserves your honesty and integrity

- How to handle adversity in the workplace—particularly, conflicts and confrontations with coworkers and supervisors—and come out a winner

Introduction

Admitting to mistakes and dealing with adversity in the workplace are two tricky issues that make us feel uncomfortable. However, you can actually come out a winner by openly admitting to a mistake and explaining the steps you plan to take to correct it. Your honesty and proactive behavior will be a positive reflection on your character.

You can also benefit by maintaining self-control during a confrontation with an angry boss, coworker, or customer, rather than becoming angry or defensive in return. How? You won't be the person who ends up regretting what they said and did during the confrontation. You will also avoid damaging a workplace relationship that can likely be salvaged.

This chapter explains how to deal with your mistakes and the adversity you may face in your job in a professional manner, which will preserve your integrity and professional reputation.

Admitting to Mistakes

It often seems to be human nature to cover up our mistakes. We fear that others will blame us for them or retaliate, that we will be expected to make restitution, or simply that we will disappoint someone or somehow be diminished in their eyes. When young children begin to lie, one of the first things they lie about involves denying that they have done something wrong. Many times, when a young child tries to lie about having done something, the lie is not particularly convincing. The parent may become more angry or frustrated by the obvious lie than by the original deed.

The same tends to apply to mistakes that one makes in the workplace. Whatever damage may be done by your mistake, the lie will only add to that damage. Failing to report an accident or mistake, or worse, deliberately trying to cover it up, can turn a minor incident into a major one. The minor incident could be an accident, something that happens to us all from time to time and does not particularly reflect on you in a negative way. However, the cover-up can cause much more devastating and lasting harm to your reputation because it is a deliberate and premeditated act.

The perfect example of the consequences of not admitting to mistakes involved former president Richard Nixon and the famous Watergate scandal. The scandal began when the news media reported attempts by Republican campaign workers to break into the headquarters of the Democratic campaign to obtain confidential information. This was against the law and, at the very least, likely to result in some adverse public reaction against the Republicans.

At first, there was no reason to believe that Nixon himself had any awareness whatsoever that underlings were committing such a relatively minor and isolated crime. Thus, the original break-in was a minor news item several steps removed from the presidency itself. Had the Nixon administration simply admitted that campaign workers had committed an illegal act, and apologized for it, the Watergate story would have stayed in the newspaper for a few days and quietly disappeared as other more interesting news stories emerged to take its place.

However, the incident snowballed and eventually led to the president's resignation—a move unprecedented in American history. The reason

that this became such a serious situation was that President Nixon and his aides tried to hide the incident by bribing people not to admit to their involvement and by deliberately destroying evidence. Thus, the American people ended up having to deal not just with poor judgment on the part of some overly zealous young official, but also with the poor judgment—and blatant dishonesty—of the country's leader. The break-in was not the scandal; the cover-up and denial were.

The Benefits of Admitting to Mistakes

When you make a mistake, especially in the workplace, you are naturally going to feel edgy and uneasy about what repercussions it may have. However, you would be much better off to direct this negative energy into finding positive ways of minimizing the damage caused by your error. If you can rectify the situation, or compensate for it in some way, you may be able to soften its impact. Sometimes simply admitting to the mistake itself can be viewed as a sign of integrity, and your honesty may draw more positive attention than the negative attention caused by the accident or mishap itself. This is especially true if your voluntary admission is coupled with an offer to rectify the situation. If you go to your boss and offer to stay late to fix the problem, and apologize for having caused it in the first place, chances are that you will be able to avoid any serious harm from the incident.

Sometimes, there is nothing more disarming to a person who is angry or who feels they have been wronged than a simple, forthright apology. If you make excuses for yourself, or deny your involvement in the incident, your supervisor will only become more angry and argumentative. However, the simple statement, "I'm sorry, I won't let it happen again," is often enough to defuse a supervisor's anger.

Of course, if your mistake involves a premeditated, unethical, or illegal activity, you may not get off so lightly. However, it is amazing how even when someone commits a minor criminal act, a simple confession and apology can sometimes reduce the consequences. When shoplifters voluntarily return to the store with merchandise they have stolen and express remorse for having taken it, charges may be dropped or reduced. Once again, you benefit from the fact that others perceive how difficult it is to come forward in these circumstances. This in itself becomes a positive reflection on your character. It

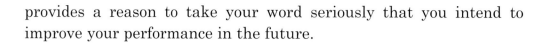

provides a reason to take your word seriously that you intend to improve your performance in the future.

Handling Adversity

Conflict in the workplace, whether with a supervisor or with a coworker, is stressful and unpleasant. It takes a physical and emotional toll. Many people respond by trying to escape from the conflict as quickly and completely as possible, sometimes at all costs. When someone is angry with you or has treated you unfairly, you might react by fighting back, or you might react by trying to get away from that person and, thereafter, trying to avoid them as much as possible.

Sometimes, both fighting back and avoidance can be unsuccessful tactics in turning the situation to your best advantage. Usually it is ill-advised to try to fight back against a supervisor, as you may be perceived as rebellious or insubordinate. In extreme cases, openly arguing with a supervisor could even lead to your dismissal. Of course, we are not talking here about physically fighting with anyone, but rather arguing, standing your ground, and refusing to concede to the other person's objectives or point of view. However, running away can be just as harmful. It may leave the situation unresolved, or cause it to be resolved in a way that is detrimental to your success.

Maintaining Self-control

So what does one do in order to handle opposition skillfully? The first requirement in trying to become a "winner" in this sort of situation is self-control. Other people may come into the situation with a loss of control. They may be angry. They may be defensive. They may even be verbally abusive. Chances are they will regret all of this later on, in calmer moments when they reflect on what happened. Sometimes the winner in a situation like this is the person who comes away with the least to regret about their own behavior. If you are the calmer one, the one more likely to think before you speak or react, you may create a situation where someone else behaves in an unacceptable way and you don't respond in kind.

If it happens that you handle yourself better in a confrontation than someone else, there are several opportunities for you to be rewarded for your behavior. For one thing, the person who lost control and said things they regret may be motivated afterward to try to make it up to

you, possibly in some indirect way without admitting to their feelings of guilt. This is particularly likely to happen if you respond the next day by not holding a grudge and by giving the person who offended you an opportunity to redeem themselves. Of course, you shouldn't come off as superior or condescending. However, simply showing that there are no hard feelings or that you are willing to let the incident pass can sometimes be the first step in forging an alliance with someone who may previously have been an adversary.

In the business world, it often happens that someone purchases a product or service that is unsatisfactory for some reason and that causes them to become upset or angry. They may return to the company or the store and begin a tirade of complaints and accusations. Business managers have learned that it is critically important how the company's employees respond to complaints and criticisms. If you become defensive or argumentative, you risk provoking a blow-up that could sever your relationship with the customer for good. However, if you admit to your mistake, apologize for it, and allow the customer to vent their frustration a little bit, you may not only retain the customer, but they may become an even better customer than they were in the past. They may regret that they lost their cool and scolded you, and they may try to make it up to you by accepting your apology and giving you another chance.

After all, it is human to want to be liked and accepted by others. Sometimes, people who are very belligerent and quick to stand up for themselves go home and wonder if they went too far. They may ask themselves if they are now disliked and disrespected by the other party involved or by anyone else who may have witnessed the incident. They may respond to this feeling of regret or insecurity by deciding to try to make it up to the other person in some way.

A good example is the high school coach who loses his temper and shouts at a player who makes a mistake during a game. If the player screams back at the coach, the coach will only become more angry and embarrassed. However, if the player simply takes the criticism, even if it seems too harsh, and does not display resentment towards the coach, afterwards the coach will calm down and may feel a little guilty. The coach may then go over and pat the player on the back and say, "Well, I know you'll do better next time." By being willing to forgive the coach, and just nodding your agreement and your willingness to

try harder, you may come away with the coach being more positively disposed to you than before the incident occurred. The coach will be grateful that you are willing to let the incident pass. In some subtle way, you may be rewarded for doing so at some point in the future.

The same sort of scenario can apply in the workplace. Even the most gruff and temperamental of bosses wants his or her employees to be loyal, respectful, and motivated. If the boss makes a mistake and steps out of line when handling a situation, you can often benefit by being clear-headed and keeping your own hurt feelings in check. By this, we do not mean bottling up your feelings and allowing yourself to be victimized. Rather, make a deliberate attempt to benefit from the situation by behaving in a positive manner, once things have calmed down and you have an opportunity to resume the interaction.

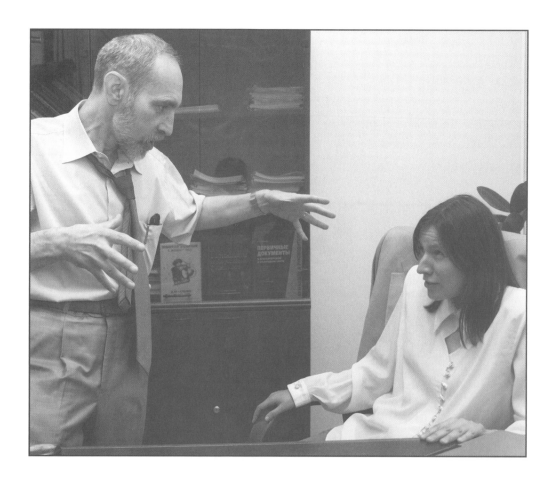

Summary

Although it is human nature to want to cover up our mistakes, doing so in the workplace can cause more damage than the mistake itself. The mistake may have been an accident or at least not deliberate behavior on your part. However, lying about the mistake or trying to cover it up can cause lasting harm to your reputation. The best way to handle mistakes in the workplace is to admit to them, apologize for them, and offer to take steps to rectify the situation.

During confrontations with angry supervisors or coworkers, arguing or refusing to concede to the other person's point of view can harm your relationship. Running away from conflicts can also be detrimental because the situation can then fester and become worse over time.

The key to handling confrontations skillfully is to maintain self-control. When the other person loses their cool and you don't, you come out a winner. Often the other person will regret what they said and did during an argument, and try to make it up to you in some way. They will be grateful that you have decided not to retaliate or hold a grudge, and your relationship is more likely to be maintained. After all, it is human to want to be liked and accepted by others.

Key Terms

Term	Definition
Adversity	A state of adverse conditions, misfortune, or calamity, or a single event that is adverse.
Conflict resolution	The process of attempting to resolve a dispute or a conflict. Successful conflict resolution occurs by listening to and providing opportunities to meet the needs of all parties, and to adequately address interests so that each party is satisfied with the outcome.
Cover-up	An attempt to conceal or disguise an action or series of actions, to try to avoid consequences or legal penalties.
Premeditation	Premeditation involves the consideration or planning of an act beforehand. It shows intent to commit that act. The term is frequently used in the context of crime to describe actions that were planned before the crime was committed.
Self-control	The exertion of an individual's restraint over their behaviors, actions, and thought processes.
Watergate scandal	Watergate is a general term for a series of political scandals, during the presidency of Richard Nixon, that began with a break-in at the Watergate hotel complex in Washington, D.C., on June 17, 1972. The attempted cover-up of the break-in ultimately led to Nixon's dramatic resignation in 1974.

CHAPTER 10

Getting Help

Highlights of the Chapter

This Chapter Covers:

- The importance of accepting help from coworkers in the workplace

- How to build and maintain alliances with coworkers

- The importance of being self-motivated and productive at work

Introduction

Most of us can't do our jobs alone. In the workplace, we often work on teams and collaborate with others to do our work. We also often rely on the knowledge, skills, and contributions of others, particularly in areas where we may lack expertise. For these reasons, it is important to build and maintain alliances with the coworkers with whom we work on a regular basis.

When we start new jobs, we are usually on a steep learning curve. Because most jobs don't come with detailed training manuals, most of what we need to learn can only be learned informally through more experienced coworkers. To learn how to do a new job, we need to be able to ask for, and accept, help from others.

This chapter discusses the importance of accepting help from others when you need it and building alliances with the coworkers with whom you work regularly. It also covers self-motivation—how you give back to a workplace by taking initiative and making your own important contribution.

Accepting Help

We all see when other people fail to accept the help that they need, but it is sometimes not so easy to see this in ourselves. The main reason people refuse to accept help is not that they don't want it, but that they somehow perceive that their willingness to take it is an admission of error or weakness on their part. We are so afraid that we will be perceived as inadequate that we often refuse the very thing that will help us become more adequate. This is the irony in many of our human relations mistakes. By our misguided actions, we actually make worse the very situation that we most dread or wish to conceal.

In the workplace, training is often provided through a combination of formal and informal channels. Sometimes only a small percentage of what we need to know in order to do our jobs is revealed to us through training manuals, classroom lectures, or other direct training methods. Most of what we learn, we learn by working with others, observing others, asking them for help, and following their corrections and directions. This refers not only to help from our supervisors, but also from our peers or coworkers.

Some people are more open to receiving help than others. Perhaps they are more secure in themselves and do not see admitting to not knowing something as an admission of failure or a personal weakness. These people have an advantage in the workplace. The fact that they are willing to accept help means that they will learn faster than those who turn it into an issue or a problem.

The other common reason for refusing to accept help is a personal antagonism between the person who needs the help and the person who is available to provide it. In the workplace, there will be some people you will like more than others. There will be some people you want to spend time with more than others. However, particularly in the early stages of your employment, when you have a lot to learn, you cannot afford to be picky about where you get the help and the informal training that you need.

You must make yourself available to the people who are in the best position to help you, those who are willing to do so, and those who have the best grasp of the knowledge or procedures that you need to learn. You must put away personality clashes and personal opinions of

other people. Instead, try to be as objective as you can about your needs and how other people can help you meet them.

The final reason why some people refuse help is simply shyness. They are afraid to ask, afraid that they will be bothering someone, afraid that they will be rebuffed. If you have these personality traits, you need to work deliberately and vigorously to suppress them to avoid putting yourself at a serious disadvantage in the workplace.

Remember one thing: everyone in the workplace is paid to be there. You are not asking coworkers to come and help you on a weekend, evening, or on their own free time. You are not taking their own personal time away from them. Especially if it is part of their job to assist you, you are not really asking them to do you any favors whatsoever. You are simply asking them to do their job and make themselves available to carry out these tasks within their job description. You need not apologize. You need not feel guilty.

Preserving Alliances

In the course of performing all of the steps we have discussed thus far, you will officially or unofficially make alliances with other people in the workplace. Your allies will be people to whom you turn for help or who turn to you for help. They are people with whom you cooperate or interact, or share a project or some degree of responsibility. An ongoing relationship with such people can be established and then maintained once the specific tasks at hand have been completed.

One common yet very subtle mistake that some people make in social interaction, especially in the workplace, is failing to keep these personal alliances active during periods when they are temporarily not being used. You can think of personal alliances like houseplants. They need to be watered every so often or they will begin to wither. In the context of workplace relationships, watering the relationship may mean stopping by someone's desk to say hello on your way back from lunch or asking someone how their day is going. Nurturing workplace alliances may also involve going to approaching a colleague when you have some free time and asking if there is anything you can do to help them with their workload, if it is appropriate for you to do so.

Another part of preserving alliances is being sensitive when other people need your help or simply need to talk to you to blow off steam or ask for your advice. A lack of sensitivity can cause hurt feelings, and can lead people to pull back from you just when you are beginning to build a rapport with them. Workplace alliances are extremely important to workplace success. To some extent this is because, as human beings, we are readily influenced by other people's opinions.

Suppose that one coworker begins to see you in a negative way, and attempts to persuade other people that you are not performing well or that you are not likeable. The alliances that you have formed are a means of intercepting those types of signals, before they are widely broadcast and accepted. If one person in the workplace doesn't like you, but three or four people do, then your friends will quickly squash any malicious gossip that may begin to circulate. When inevitable conflicts or confrontations do arise, then the alliances you have formed will provide a "safety net" of other people who will stand up for you, who will vouch for you, and who may even be willing to protest if you are unfairly treated or falsely accused.

Furthermore, even if there is no outright confrontation, the simple fact that someone perceives that other people are loyal to you and respect you may cause them to reconsider their own negative opinion of you. People don't often like to be in a minority of one. Thus, the fact that you are obviously on good terms with others will make potential opponents think twice about opposing you, or even wishing to oppose you.

There are all sorts of career self-interest reasons for forming alliances in the workplace. There is also a simpler and more general one. Isolation is an unpleasant experience for most human beings. We are happier in almost any setting if we are part of a group that accepts us and helps provide us with a sense of identity. Workplace alliances help to fuel these positive feelings about one's job experience.

Sometimes workplace alliances need to be fostered outside of the workplace, by being willing to accept invitations to attend parties or social events, if it is appropriate for you to do so. If the department is going out to eat on the last afternoon before the holidays and you refuse to tag along, you may do harm to some of the alliances that you have begun to establish, perhaps without meaning to do so. Just as you must make it a priority to spend time with your spouse or with

your children, you should make it a priority to spend some meaningful time with the people in the workplace with whom you have built up positive relationships.

Self-motivation

So far in this chapter, we have stressed the importance of leveraging relationships in the workplace to get assistance and job training from colleagues and to preserve alliances with them. It is also important to give back to our colleagues, the teams on which we work, and to our employers in general, by making our own important contribution. Each of us has a unique mix of knowledge, skills, and expertise that allow us to become valuable employees. But this can only be achieved if we are motivated to do it.

One of the most serious mistakes that people make in the workplace, particularly when they are first starting out, is that they fail to convey a sense of being self-motivated. They may show up with their hands in their pockets waiting for someone to tell them what to do. They feel that their role is to be subservient. They interpret that as meaning that the boss will give out instructions and they will follow them, but in the meantime they will just sit back and wait for instructions.

However, in the majority of situations, this is not what an employer is looking for. Yes, they want you to take instructions and they expect you to make sure that you understand what is required before you undertake any task. However, after a point, they would like you to come to work with the attitude that you are going to find the best way to use your time to accomplish what the employer needs done that day. You are not simply going to wait for someone to come in and tell you what to do at every moment.

One of the problems with not being self-motivated is that you may seem lazy. You may give your boss the impression that you are going to work only when he or she is watching you or asking you to do a specific task. It may seem to your boss that, at other times, you prefer to just sit there and do nothing. By being self-motivated, you can keep yourself active and energetic, and this reflects positively on your character. If no one has given you a specific assignment, find something productive to do. This creates an impression that you are hard-working.

Being self-motivated and productive also helps to make the time pass more quickly. As mentioned earlier in this text, there is nothing more tedious than sitting around in the workplace waiting for something to happen. Those are the longest, slowest and most frustrating work days that you will have to deal with. Once you become engaged in an activity and it captures your full attention, you will find the minutes and hours ticking by at a much more rapid rate. You will be happier, and your employer will be impressed that you don't wait for instructions from someone else to get busy and do useful work.